POLISH

Verbs & Essentials
of Grammar

Oscar E. Swan

New York Chicago San Francisco Lisbon London Madrid Mexico City
Milan New Delhi San Juan Seoul Singapore Sydney Toronto

Library of Congress Cataloging-in-Publication Data

Swan, Oscar E.
    Polish verbs & essentials of grammar / by Oscar E. Swan. — 1st ed.
        p.   cm.
    Includes index.
    ISBN 0-07-159746-8 (alk. paper)
    1. Polish language—Grammar.   I. Title.   II. Title: Polish verbs
and essentials of grammar.

    PG6105.S893   2008
    491.8′582421—dc22   2008012716

9 10 11 12 13 14 15 16 17   DOC   21 20 19 18 17 16

ISBN 978-0-07-159746-3
MHID   0-07-159746-8

McGraw-Hill books are available at special quantity discounts to use
as premiums and sales promotions or for use in corporate training
programs. To contact a representative, please visit the Contact Us pages
at www.myprofessional.com.

This book is printed on acid-free paper.

Contents

Introduction

The Polish language belongs to the Slavic group of Indo-European languages. It is most closely allied with Slovak and Czech, with many features in common with Ukrainian. The earliest Polish writing dates to the 14th and 15th centuries. Polish attained status as a means of sophisticated literary expression in the 16th century, and attained full maturity as a language fulfilling all social functions in the 17th and 18th centuries. Contemporary Standard Polish, based in the main on the Warsaw variant of the language, is spoken or at least understood throughout Poland.

The country of Poland (officially **Rzeczpospolita Polska,** the Republic of Poland) is situated to the east of Germany and to the north of the Czech Republic and Slovakia. To the north is the Baltic Sea, and to the east are Lithuania, Belarus, and Ukraine. The contemporary borders of Poland were determined following World War II at the Potsdam Conference of 1945. Poland has an area of 120,700 square miles and a population of 38.5 million. The capital of Poland (and its largest city) is Warsaw, with a population of about 1.7 million. Other major cities are Bydgoszcz, Gdańsk, Katowice, Kraków, Łódź, Lublin, Poznań, Szczecin, and Wrocław. Nearly the entire population speaks Polish, and the vast majority of those professing a religion are Roman Catholic. A sizable number of Poles live outside the country in English-speaking countries: in North America, Australia, and—especially recently—the British Isles.

Polish Verbs & Essentials of Grammar is intended for use as a short reference and review grammar at any level of Polish language study, from beginning to advanced. It summarizes the grammar usually covered in the first two years of study. Chapter 11 lists more than 500 basic Polish verbs and provides details of their conjugation.

Abbreviations

1pl.	first-person plural
3pl.	third-person plural
3sg.	third-person singular
acc.	accusative case
conj.	conjunction
dat.	dative case
det.	determinate verb
fem.	feminine gender
gen.	genitive case
imp.	imperative
impf.	imperfective aspect
indet.	indeterminate verb
inf.	infinitive
instr.	instrumental case
intr.	intransitive
irreg.	irregular
lit.	literally
loc.	locative case
masc.	masculine gender
masc.pers.	masculine personal
neut.	neuter gender
nom.	nominative case
p., pers.	person, personal
pf.	perfective aspect
pl.	plural
refl.	reflexive
sg.	singular
subord.	subordinating
tr.	transitive
voc.	vocative case

1. The Polish Alphabet and Sounds

The Polish alphabet has 32 letters:

a	f	m	ś
ą	g	n	t
b	h	ń	u
c	i	o	w
ć	j	ó	y
d	k	p	z
e	l	r	ź
ę	ł	s	ż

Sound Values of the Letters

Letter/ Combination	Approximate English Sound	Example Polish Words
a	f*a*ther	**tak** *thus, so, yes,* **raz** *once*
ą	d*om*e	**są** *they are,* **wąż** *snake*

The sound **ą** is pronounced like *om*, except that the lips and tongue are not completely closed to pronounce the *m*, leaving a nasal resonance instead.

b	*b*ig	**bok** *side,* **aby** *so that*
bi	*b*eautiful	**bieg** *course, run, race,* **tobie** *to you*
c	fi*ts*	**co** *what,* **taca** *tray,* **noc** *night*
ch	*h*all	**chata** *cottage,* **ucho** *ear,* **dach** *roof*

The sound **ch** is much raspier and noisier than English *h*.

ci	*ch*eek	**ciasto** *cake,* **cicho** *quiet*
cz	*ch*alk	**czas** *time,* **tęcza** *rainbow,* **gracz** *player*
ć	*ch*eek	**nićmi** *thread* (instr.pl.), **choć** *although*

The letter **ć** and letter combination **ci** are pronounced the same. The combination **ci** is used before a vowel. The letter **c** before **i** is pronounced like **ć/ci**. The sound of **ć/ci**, pronounced with the mouth in the position for English *y,* is different from that of **cz**, which is pronounced with the mouth in the position for English *r*.

d	*do*	**data** *date*, **lada** *counter*
dz	o*dds*	**cudzy** *foreign*, **wodze** *reins*
dzi	*j*eans	**dziadek** *grandfather*, **ludzie** *people*
dź	*j*eans	**wiedźma** *witch*, **ludźmi** *people* (instr.pl.)
dż	*j*aw	**dżez** *jazz*, **radża** *rajah*

The letter **dź** and letter combination **dzi** are pronounced the same. The combination **dzi** is used before a vowel. The letter combination **dz** before **i** is pronounced like **dź/dzi**. The sound of **dź/dzi**, pronounced with the mouth in the position for English *y*, is different from that of **dż**, which is pronounced with the mouth in the position for English *r*.

e	*g*et	**Edek** *Eddie*, **ten** *this* (masc.), **ale** *but*
ę	*sen*se	**gęś** *goose*, **tęsknić** *long for*

The sound **ę** is pronounced like *em*, except that the lips and tongue are not completely closed to pronounce the *m*, leaving a nasal resonance instead. At the end of a word, the sound **ę** is normally pronounced the same as **e**: **naprawdę** "naprawde."

f	*f*elt	**farba** *paint*, **lufa** *rifle barrel*, **blef** *bluff*
g	*g*et	**guma** *rubber*, **noga** *leg, foot*
gi	a*gu*e	**giełda** *stock market*, **magiel** *mangle*
h	*h*all	**hak** *hook*, **aha** *aha!*

The letter **h** is pronounced the same as **ch**; it appears mainly in words of foreign origin.

i	ch*ee*k	**igła** *needle*, **list** *letter*
j	*y*ou, bo*y*	**jak** *as*, **zając** *hare*, **raj** *paradise*
k	*k*eg	**kot** *cat*, **oko** *eye*, **rok** *year*
ki	li*ke y*ou	**kiedy** *when*, **takie** *such* (neut.)
l	*l*ove	**las** *forest*, **fala** *wave*, **dal** *distance*
ł	*w*ag, bo*w*	**łeb** *animal head*, **ołówek** *pencil*, **był** *he was*
m	*m*oth	**mama** *mama*, **tom** *volume*
mi	har*m y*ou	**miara** *measure*, **ziemia** *earth*
n	*n*ot	**noc** *night*, **ono** *it*, **pan** *sir*
ni	ca*ny*on	**nie** *no, not*, **nigdy** *never*
ń	ca*ny*on	**hańba** *disgrace*, **koń** *horse*

The letter **ń** and letter combination **ni** are pronounced the same. The combination **ni** is used before a vowel. The letter **n** before **i** is pronounced like **ń/ni**.

o	p*o*ke	**osa** *wasp*, **pot** *sweat*, **okno** *window*
ó	t*oo*t	**ból** *pain*, **ołówek** *pencil*

The letter **ó** is pronounced the same as **u**.

p	*p*u*p*	**pas** *belt, strap,* **łapa** *paw,* **cap** *billy goat*
pi	sto*p y*ou	**piana** *foam,* **łapie** *he catches*
r	a*rr*iba (*Spanish*)	**rada** *advice,* **kara** *punishment,* **dar** *gift*

The letter **r** is pronounced by trilling the tip of the tongue, as in Spanish, Italian, and Russian. However, it is less strongly trilled than in these other languages.

rz	plea*s*ure	**rzeka** *river,* **morze** *sea*

The letter combination **rz** is pronounced the same as **ż**, more or less as in *pleasure*; see below.

s	*s*ad	**sam** *the same* (masc.), **rasa** *breed,* **pas** *belt*
si	*sh*eep	**siano** *hay,* **sito** *sieve*
sz	*sh*ark	**szal** *frenzy,* **dusza** *soul*
ś	*sh*eep	**śpi** *he sleeps,* **kwaśny** *sour,* **oś** *axle*

The letter **ś** and letter combination **si** are pronounced the same. The combination **si** is used before a vowel. The letter **s** before **i** is pronounced like **ś/si**. The sound of **ś/si**, pronounced with the mouth in the position for English *y*, is different from that of **sz**, which is pronounced with the mouth in the position for English *r*.

t	*t*op	**tam** *there,* **data** *date,* **kot** *cat*
u	t*oo*t	**but** *shoe,* **tu** *here,* **ucho** *ear*
w	*v*at	**wata** *cotton wadding,* **kawa** *coffee*
y	b*i*t	**dym** *smoke,* **ty** *you* (sg.)
z	*z*oo	**zupa** *soup,* **faza** *phase*
zi	a*z*ure	**ziarno** *grain,* **zima** *winter*
ź	a*z*ure	**wyraźny** *distinct,* **źle** *badly*
ż	plea*s*ure	**żaba** *frog,* **plaża** *beach*

The letter **ź** and letter combination **zi** are pronounced the same. The combination **zi** is used before a vowel. The letter **z** before **i** is pronounced like **ź/zi**. The sound of **ź/zi**, pronounced with the mouth in the position for English *y*, is different from that of **ż/rz**, which is pronounced with the mouth in the position for English *r*.

Notes on Spelling and Pronunciation

1. The Polish alphabet has no **q**, **v**, or **x**, although these letters may be found in transcriptions of foreign names and in a few borrowed words, for example, **status quo**, **video**, and **pan X** *Mr. X* "iks."

2. The Polish oral (non-nasal) vowels, **a, e, i, o, u/ó, y**, are pronounced with exactly the same short length, achieved by not moving the tongue or lips after the onset of the vowel—unlike, for example, the English vowel sounds **ee** (*knee*), **oe** (*toe*), and **oo** (*boot*). Only the nasal vowels, **ą** and **ę**, are pronounced long, the length being due to rounding the lips and pronouncing the glide *w* at the end: **Są** is pronounced "sow," except that the glide is nasalized.

3. Polish consonants may be pronounced slightly differently, according to their position in a word. Most importantly, voiced consonants **b, d, dz, g, rz, w, z, ź, ż** are pronounced as unvoiced consonants (**p, t, c, k, sz, f, s, ś, sz**, respectively) in final position. For example, **paw** is pronounced "paf," and **chodź** is pronounced "choć."

Voiced	b	d	dz	dź	g	rz	w	z	ź	ż
Voiceless	p	t	c	ć	k	sz	f	s	ś	sz

4. The letters **ą** and **ę** are usually pronounced like **on/om** and **en/em**, respectively, before consonants. For example, **ląd** is pronounced "lont," **dąb** is pronounced "domp," **tępy** is pronounced "tempy," and **dęty** is pronounced "denty." Before **ć** and **dź**, **ą** and **ę** are pronounced as **oń** and **eń**, respectively: **lądzie** "lońdzie," **chęć** "cheńć." Before **k** and **g**, **ą** and **ę** may be pronounced as **o** and **e**, respectively, plus the English *ng* sound: **mąka** "mongka," **potęga** "potenga." The vowels **ą** and **ę** are usually denasalized before **l** and **ł**: **zdjął** "zdjoł," **zdjęli** "zdjeli."

5. The stress in a Polish word falls on the next-to-last syllable: **sprawa** (SPRA-wa), **Warszawa** (War-SZA-wa), **gospodarka** (go-spo-DAR-ka), **zadowolony** (za-do-wo-LO-ny). As these examples show, Polish syllables tend to divide after a vowel. Words that end in **-yka** take stress on the preceding syllable (**matematyka** (ma-te-MA-ty-ka), **muzyka** (MU-zy-ka)), as does **uniwersytet** (u-ni-WER-sy-tet). The past tense endings **-yśmy/-iśmy** and **-yście/-iście** do not cause a shift in stress: **byłyśmy** (BY-łyś-my).

Spelling Rules

1. So-called kreska consonants (**ć, dź, ń, ś, ż**) are spelled with an acute mark only at the end of words and before consonants; otherwise, they are spelled **c, dz, n, s, z** plus **i**: **dzień** (dźeń), **nie** (ńe). Before the vowel **i** itself, no extra **i** is used: **ci** (ći, *to you*).

2. Certain instances of **b, p, w, f, m** are latently soft (**b', p', w', f', m'**), meaning that they are treated as soft (in effect, as kreska consonants) before vowels. They are spelled **b, p, w, f, m** plus **i**; compare **paw** *peacock* and its plural **pawie** (paw'-e).

3. The letter **y** is used only after a hard consonant (see below) or after **c, cz, dz, rz, sz, ż**. The letter **i** after the consonants **c, dz, n, s, z** always indicates the pronunciations **ć, dź, ń, ś, ź**, respectively. Only **i** (never **y**) is used after **l** or **j**.

4. The letter **e** is usually separated from a preceding **k** or **g** by **i**, indicating a change before **e** of **k** to **k'** and **g** to **g'**: **jakie** (jak'e), **drogie** (drog'e).

5. The letter **j** is dropped after a vowel before **i**: **stoję** *I stand,* but **stoisz** *you stand;* **mój** *my,* but **moi** *my* (masc.pers.pl.).

Sound Changes

1. In describing word formation, some consonants are considered hard (H) and others soft (S):

H	p	b	f	w	m	t	d	s	z	n	ł	r	k	g	ch
S1	p'	b'	f'	w'	m'	ć	dź	ś	ź	ń	l	rz	c	dz	sz/ś	j
S2	cz	ż													

Hard consonants soften before certain endings. For example, **r** becomes **rz** before the locative singular ending **-'e**: **biurze** (**biur-** + **-'e**, from **biuro** *office*).

As noted, the consonants **b, p, w, f, m** at the end of a word may turn out to be soft when not at the end of a word; compare **paw** *peacock* and its plural **pawie** *peacocks.*

2. One often observes vowel changes within Polish words when endings are added to them. The most important of these changes involve an alternation between **ó** and **o**, **ą** and **ę**, **io/ia** and **ie**, and **e** and — (null) (fleeting, or mobile, **e**). These changes may be observed in the singular and plural forms of the following nouns: **stół** *table* ~ **stoły** *tables,* **ząb** *tooth* ~ **zęby** *teeth,* **sąsiad** *neighbor* ~ **sąsiedzi** *neighbors,* **sen** *dream* ~ **sny** *dreams,* **pies** *dog* ~ **psy** *dogs.*

2. Nouns

Preliminaries

Lack of Articles

Polish has no indefinite and definite articles analogous to English *a/an* and *the*. A noun is interpreted as definite or indefinite on the basis of context. Hence, **dom** may be interpreted as *a house* or *the house*.

Noun Gender

A Polish noun has one of three genders: masculine, feminine, or neuter. Grammatical gender has nothing to do with natural gender, that is, the "sex" of a noun. It is mainly of importance for purposes of grammatical agreement. For example, feminine nouns require that a modifying adjective have feminine endings, as in **dobra lampa** *a good lamp*; compare this with masculine **dobry stół** *a good table* and neuter **dobre krzesło** *a good chair*. While names for males are masculine in gender, names for females are feminine, and names for barnyard animals often have natural gender (for example, **krowa** *cow* and **byk** *bull*), other objects in the world are assigned gender in an arbitrary way. For example, **nos** *nose* is masculine, while **głowa** *head* is feminine, and **słońce** *sun* is neuter, while **księżyc** *moon* is masculine.

Noun Stems

A noun may end in a consonant or a vowel; if it ends in a vowel, the stem of the noun, to which endings are added, is obtained by removing the vowel, yielding a consonant stem. For example, the stem of **głowa** *head* is **głow-**, while the stem of **nos** *nose* is **nos-**. The stem of **mieszkanie** *apartment* is **mieszkań-** (tracing in reverse the spelling rule **ń** + **e** = **nie**).

Masculine Nouns

Masculine nouns usually end in a consonant: **nos** *nose*, **stół** *table*, **hotel** *hotel*, **piec** *stove*, **mąż** *husband*. Names for males may end in -**a**: **kolega** *colleague*, **dentysta** *dentist*, even **mężczyzna** *man*. Often, masculine nouns have different stems, depending on whether they have an ending or not: **stół** *table* ~ **stoły** *tables*, **mąż** *husband* ~ **mężowie** *husbands*.

Plural of Masculine Non-Personal Nouns

Masculine non-personal nouns ending in a hard consonant (see Chapter 1, Sound Changes) usually form the plural by adding **-y**: **nos** *nose* → **nosy**, **stół** *table* → **stoły**. After **k** or **g**, the **-y** becomes **-i**: **czek** *check* → **czeki**. Masculine non-personal nouns ending in a soft consonant usually form the plural by adding **-e**: **hotel** *hotel* → **hotele**, **piec** *stove* → **piece**.

Plural of Masculine Personal Nouns

Masculine personal nouns often take special endings in the plural. If the stem consonant is hard, the ending is usually **-i/-y** and the preceding consonant is softened: **student** *student* → **studenci**, **Polak** *Pole* → **Polacy**. If the stem consonant is soft, the ending is usually **-e**, that is, like non-personal nouns: **nauczyciel** *teacher* → **nauczyciele**. With titles and relation names, the ending **-owie** is often used: **pan** *sir* → **panowie**, **profesor** *professor* → **profesorowie**, **mąż** *husband* → **mężowie**; **brat** *brother* → **bracia** is an exception. A few masculine personal nouns have a plural in **-'e**: **Amerykanin** *American* → **Amerykanie**.

Feminine Nouns

Most feminine nouns end in **-a**: **lampa** *lamp*, **kobieta** *woman*, **krowa** *cow*, **siostra** *sister*, **mama** *mama*, **torba** *bag*, **ulica** *street*. Some feminine nouns end in a soft consonant: **twarz** *face*, **kość** *bone*, **noc** *night*, **rzecz** *thing*, **kolej** *railroad*. A few feminine personal nouns end in **-i**: **gospodyni** *landlady*. The noun **osoba** *person* is feminine, whether it refers to a man or a woman.

Plural of Feminine Nouns

Feminine nouns follow approximately the same rules as masculine nouns in forming the plural. Nouns ending in a hard consonant add **-y**: **kobiety** *women*, **krowy** *cows*, **siostry** *sisters*, **torby** *bags*. After **k** or **g**, the **-y** becomes **-i**: **noga** *leg* → **nogi**. Feminine nouns whose stems end in a soft consonant usually form the plural by adding **-e**: **koleje** *rails*, **ulice** *streets*, **twarze** *faces*. Some feminine nouns that do not end in **-a** add **-y/-i**: **rzeczy** *things*, **kości** *bones*.

Neuter Nouns

Neuter nouns end in **-o** or (after soft consonants) **-e**: **mydło** *soap*, **koło** *wheel*, **piwo** *beer*, **morze** *sea*, **pole** *field*, **zdanie** *opinion*. Exceptions are neuter nouns like **imię** *name* and **zwierzę** *animal*, which end in **ę**. Some neuter nouns, borrowed from Latin, end in **-um**: **muzeum** *museum*.

Plural of Neuter Nouns

Neuter nouns form the plural by adding -a: **koła** *wheels,* **piwa** *beers,* **morza** *seas,* **pola** *fields,* **zdania** *opinions.* The plurals of **imię** *name* and **zwierzę** *animal* are **imiona** and **zwierzęta**, respectively. The plural of **muzeum** *museum* is **muzea**. The noun **dziecko** *child* is neuter; its plural is **dzieci**. The nouns **oko** *eye* and **ucho** *ear* also have exceptional plurals: **oczy** and **uszy**, respectively.

Names for People and Their Plural Forms

Singular	English Translation	Plural
babcia	grandmother	babcie
brat	brother	bracia
chłopiec	boy	chłopcy
ciocia	aunt	ciocie
córka	daughter	córki
człowiek	man, human	ludzie
dziadek	grandfather	dziadkowie
dziecko	child	dzieci
dziewczyna	girl	dziewczyny
kobieta	woman	kobiety
kolega (masc.)	colleague	koledzy
koleżanka (fem.)	colleague	koleżanki
krewna (fem.)	relative	krewne
krewny (masc.)	relative	krewni
matka	mother	matki
mężczyzna	man	mężczyźni
mąż	husband	mężowie
narzeczona	fiancée	narzeczone
narzeczony	fiancé	narzeczeni
ojciec	father	ojcowie
osoba	person	osoby
przyjaciel (masc.)	friend	przyjaciele
przyjaciółka (fem.)	friend	przyjaciółki
sąsiad (masc.)	neighbor	sąsiedzi
sąsiadka (fem.)	neighbor	sąsiadki
siostra	sister	siostry
syn	son	synowie
ta pani	that lady	te panie
ten pan	that gentleman	ci panowie
wujek	uncle	wujkowie
znajoma (fem.)	acquaintance	znajome
znajomy (masc.)	acquaintance	znajomi

Cases and Case Use

Polish nouns have different forms for expressing *grammatical case,* related to the function of a noun in a sentence. For each gender, there are endings for the nominative, genitive, dative, accusative, instrumental, locative, and vocative cases—seven cases in all—in both singular and plural. In general, the nominative case is used to express the *subject* of a sentence, the dative to express the *indirect object* (to or for whom something is done), and the accusative the *direct object* (the item perceived by or acted on by the subject). The instrumental expresses the *means* by which something is done (for example, *ride by train, write with a pen*). The genitive expresses *possession* and most meanings of *of* (for example, *husband of my sister, top of the mountain, end of the film*). The locative is used with certain prepositions, especially prepositions expressing the simple location senses of *in, at,* and *on.* The vocative is used in *direct address*; it is usually replaced by the nominative.

Here is a summary of the main Polish case uses. The pronominal questions with the corresponding forms of **co** *what* and **kto** *who* are given next to the case name.

Nominative Case (*co? kto?*)

The nominative case is used:

1. For the subject of a finite verb

   Jan kocha Marię.   *Jan* loves Maria.
   Maria kocha Jana.   *Maria* loves Jan.

2. For the subject of existential *be*

   Jan jest w domu.   *Jan* is at home.
   Czy jest *szynka*?   Is there *any ham*?

3. For the complement of the identifying phrase **to jest/są** *that is/those are*

   To jest *nowe muzeum*.   That is *a new museum.*
   To są *moje okulary*.   Those are *my eyeglasses.*

4. For the complement of a naming phrase

   Jestem *Adam Wolak*.   I am *Adam Wolak.*

Genitive Case (*czego? kogo?*)

The genitive case is used:

1. To express almost all senses of *of,* including possession

   To jest dom *mojego przyjaciela*.   That's the house *of my friend.*
   To jest koniec *pierwszej lekcji*.   That's the end *of the first lesson.*

2. For the object of certain prepositions, including **do** *to,* **bez** *without,* **dla** *for,* **z** *from,* **out of,** **od** *from,* and **u** *at a person's place.* For a more complete list of prepositions, see Chapter 7.

Idę do *kina* bez *was*.	I'm going to *the movies* without *you.*
Tu jest coś dla *ciebie*.	Here is something for *you.*
Wracam z *Warszawy*.	I'm returning from *Warsaw.*
On jest starszy od *siostry*.	He is younger than *(his) sister.*

3. For the object of negated transitive verbs. Compare the following pairs of sentences:

Mam *nowy telewizor*.	I have *a new television set* (acc.).
Nie mam *nowego telewizora*.	I don't have *a new television set* (gen.).
Już skończyłem *drugą lekcję*.	I have already finished *the second lesson* (acc.).
Jeszcze nie zacząłem *drugiej lekcji*.	I haven't begun *the second lesson* (gen.) yet.

4. For the complement of the negative existential constructions **nie ma** *there isn't,* **nie było** *there wasn't,* and **nie będzie** *there won't be*

Nie ma *masła*.	There is no *butter.*
***Marii* jeszcze nie ma.**	*Maria* isn't here yet.

5. For the object of certain verbs, for example, **szukać** *look for*

Szukam *ciekawego prezentu*.	I'm looking for *an interesting present.*

Here is a list of common verbs that take the genitive case:

bać się	be afraid of
napić się	have a drink of
nienawidzić	hate
pilnować	look after, tend, mind
potrzebować	need
słuchać	listen to
spodziewać się	expect
szukać	look for
uczyć	teach
uczyć się	study
używać	use, make use of
wymagać	require, demand
zapomnieć	forget
życzyć sobie	wish, desire

6. For nouns in quantities of five or more (gen.pl.). Compare the following pairs of phrases:

jedno świeże jajko	one fresh egg
pięć *świeżych jajek*	five *fresh eggs* (gen.pl.)
jedna szeroka ulica	one wide street
sześć *szerokich ulic*	six *wide streets* (gen.pl.)
jeden nowy hotel	one new hotel
siedem *nowych hoteli*	seven *new hotels* (gen.pl.)

7. For nouns in expressions of weights and measures and with quantifiers like **dużo, mało**, and **trochę**

kieliszek *wina*	a glass *of wine* (gen.sg.)
szklanka *wody*	a glass *of water* (gen.sg.)
dużo *domów*	a lot *of houses* (gen.pl.)
mało *mieszkań*	not many *apartments* (gen.pl.)
trochę *sera*	a little *cheese* (gen.sg.)

8. To express the sense of *some, a bit of*

Nalać ci *herbaty*?	Should I pour you *some tea*?

9. As the genitive of time

tej nocy	on that night
piątego stycznia	on the fifth of January

Dative Case (*czemu? komu?*)

The dative case is used:

1. To express the senses of *to* and *for* a person, especially the indirect object (naming the recipient or beneficiary of an action), or sometimes the person negatively affected by an action

Kup *mi* **coś.**	Buy *me* something.
Zepsułem *ci* **samochód.**	I've ruined your car *for you*.

2. For a person to whom communication is directed

Powiedz *mi* **coś.**	Tell *me* something.

3. For the complement in constructions with verbs like **podobać się** *be pleasing to*, **pomagać** *help*, **powodzić się** *be successful for*, **smakować** *taste*, and **dziwić się** *be surprised at*

Twój kolega podoba *mi* **się.**	Your colleague is attractive *to me*.
Muszę *mu* **pomagać.**	I have to help *him*.

Dobrze *mu* się powodzi.	*He* is doing very well.
Dziwię się *tobie*.	I'm surprised *at you.*
Zdaje *ci* się.	It seems that way *to you.*

4. For the complement of impersonal adjectives

Jest *mi* zimno.	*I* am cold. (It's cold *to me.*)
Nam jest łatwo.	It's easy *for us.*

5. For the object of the prepositions **dzięki** *due to,* **ku** *toward,* **przeciw(ko)** *against,* and **wbrew** *despite*

Wszystko, co wiem, to dzięki *tobie.*	Everything I know is thanks to *you.*
Nie mam nic przeciwko *temu.*	I don't have anything against *that.*

Accusative Case (*co? kogo?*)

The accusative case is used:

1. For the complement of transitive verbs

Mam *brata* i *siostrę.*	I have *a brother* and *sister.*
Chcę kupić *ser, masło,* i *cytrynę.*	I want to buy *cheese, butter,* and *a lemon.*
Chciałbym poznać *twoich przyjaciół.*	I'd like to meet *your friends.*

This use of the accusative is called the direct object use. In general, the accusative is used after a verb unless there is a specific reason to use another case.

2. For the object of various verb + preposition phrasal combinations, for example, **czekać na** *wait for,* **patrzyć na** *look at,* **pytać o** *ask about,* **martwić się o** *worry about,* and **dbać o** *look after, care about*

Czekam na *moją córkę.*	I'm waiting for *my daughter.*
O *co* pytasz?	*What* are you asking about?
Dbam o *kondycję.*	I see to *my fitness.*

3. For the object of the prepositions **przez** *across, through, by (means of),* **za** in the meanings *in/after a period of time* and *in exchange for,* **na** in the meanings *for* and *to,* and **w** in the meaning *into* and in various other expressions.

Pan Józef został zaangażowany przez *pana Kowalczyka.*	Jozef was hired by *Mr. Kowalczyk.*
Będę gotowy za *minutę.*	I'll be ready in *a minute.*
Dziękuję za *prezent.*	Thanks for *the present.*

Idziemy do Warszawy na	We're going to Warsaw to *a*
konferencję.	*conference.*
Wchodzimy w *las*.	We're entering *the forest*.
Wyjeżdżam do Krakowa w	I'm going to Krakow on *Monday*.
poniedziałek.	

4. For the object of the usually instrumental prepositions **między**, **nad**, **pod**, **przed**, and **za** in the sense of *motion to*

Jedziemy nad *morze*.	We are going to *the sea*.
Taksówka podjechała pod	The taxi drove up to *the house*.
***dom*.**	

5. To express duration of time

Pracowałem tam *jedną*	I worked there *(for) one hour*.
***godzinę*.**	

Instrumental Case (*czym? kim?*)

The instrumental case is used:

1. For predicate nouns after linking verbs like **być** *be* and **zostać** *become*

Jestem *farmakologiem*.	I am *a pharmacologist*.
Ona jest *gwiazdą filmową*.	She is *a movie star*.
On został *prezydentem*.	He became *president*.

2. To express *by means of* (agent) and *by way of* (path, route)

Jedziemy tam *moim*	We're going there *in my car*.
***samochodem*.**	
Piszę *nowym długopisem*.	I'm writing with *a new ballpoint pen*.
Niech pan idzie *tą ulicą* do	Go along *this street* to the corner.
rogu.	

3. To express body movement to accompany an action

Ona machnęła *ręką*.	She waved *(with) her hand*.
On zareagował *uśmiechem*.	He reacted *with a smile*.

4. To express abstract causes

Byłem zaskoczony jego	I was surprised *by his sincerity*.
***szczerością*.**	

5. To express *with respect to*

On może jest starszy *wiekiem*	He may be older *with respect to age,*
ale nie *usposobieniem*.	but not *deportment*.

6. To express seasons and periods of time

zimą	in the winter
nocą	at night
wieczorem	in the evening

7. For the object of the static-location prepositions **między** *between,* **nad** *over,* **pod** *under,* **przed** *before,* **z** *with,* and **za** *behind*

Siedzę pod *lipą.*	I'm sitting under *a linden tree.*
Idę na koncert z *moimi dobrymi przyjaciółmi.*	I'm going to a concert with *my good friends.*

8. For the object of certain verbs, for example, **interesować się** *be interested in,* **kierować** *direct,* **zajmować się** *be busy with,* and **władać** *have power over, master*

Interesuję się *muzyką klasyczną.*	I'm interested in *classical music.*
Matka zajmuje się *domem* i *dziećmi.*	Mother takes care of *the house* and *children.*
Trzeba władać *tym przypadkiem gramatycznym.*	One must master *this grammatical case.*

Locative Case (*o czym? o kim?*)

The locative case is used after the prepositions **w** *in,* **na** *on, at,* **o** *about,* **po** *after,* and **przy** *near, during, while.*

On jest teraz w *domu.*	He is at *home* now.
Muszę kupić znaczki na *poczcie.*	I have to buy stamps at *the post office.*
Po *zajęciach* idziemy na kolację.	After *classes,* we are going to supper.
Biblioteka stoi przy *ulicy Pięknej.*	The library is on *Piekna Street.*

See above for uses of **w**, **na**, **o**, and **po** with the accusative.

Vocative Case

Usually, the nominative case functions as a de facto vocative.

***Paweł,* chodź tu!**	*Pawel,* come here!

In conjunction with titles, however, the vocative is obligatory.

Dzień dobry, *panie profesorze*!	Hello, *professor*!

The vocative case is usually used with diminutive (affectionate) forms of first names: **Kasiu! Grzesiu!** With other first names, it is optional.

The Main Kinds of Noun Phrases and the Cases They Usually Take

1. Subject of a verb (nominative)

   Ewa uczy się.   *Ewa* is studying.

2. Subject of existential *be* (nominative; genitive if negated)

   Ewa jest.   *Ewa* (nom.) is here.
   Ewy nie ma.   *Ewa* (gen.) is not here.

3. Complement in an identity sentence (nominative)

   Ewa to (jest) *moja dobra*   Ewa is *my good friend.*
   przyjaciółka.
   To (są) *nasi nowi sąsiedzi.*   Those are *our new neighbors.*

4. Predicate noun after a linking verb (instrumental)

   Ewa jest *interesującą osobą.*   Ewa is *an interesting person.*

5. Direct object (accusative; genitive if negated)

   Ewa kupuje *nową bluzkę* (acc.).   Ewa buys *a new blouse.*
   Ewa nie chce kupić *tej bluzki*   Ewa doesn't want to buy *that blouse.*
      (gen.).

6. Oblique object (various cases, depending on the verb)

   Ewa pilnuje *dziecka.*   Ewa looks after *the child* (gen.).
   Ewa pomaga *Adamowi.*   Ewa helps *Adam* (dat.).
   Ewa zajmuje się *domem.*   Ewa takes care of *the house* (instr.).

7. Complement of a verb + preposition combination (various cases, depending on the verb and preposition)

   Ewa czeka na *Adama.*   Ewa waits for *Adam* (acc.).
   Ewa cieszy się z *prezentu.*   Ewa is glad for *the present* (gen.).
   Ewa zastanawia się nad   Ewa considers *the problem* (instr.).
      problemem.
   Ewa myśli o *swoim psie.*   Ewa thinks about *her dog* (loc.).

8. Indirect object or complement of a verb of information transfer (dative)

   Ewa mówi coś *Adamowi.*   Ewa says something *to Adam.*

9. Beneficiary (dative OR **dla** + genitive)

   Pozmywałem *ci* naczynia.   I washed the dishes *for you* (dat.).
   Zrób to *dla mnie.*   Do that *for me* (gen.).

10. Phrase of means (instrumental OR **przy pomocy** + genitive)

Ewa jeździ do pracy *autobusem.*   Ewa goes to work *by bus* (instr.).
On chodzi *przy pomocy laski.*   He walks *with the aid of a cane* (gen.).

11. Complement of locational preposition (usually preposition + locative or instrumental, depending on the preposition; with people, **u** + genitive)

Ewa mieszka *w Warszawie.*   Ewa lives *in Warsaw* (loc.).
Byłem *na wystawie.*   I was *at an exhibition* (loc.).
Ewa stoi *przed domem.*   Ewa stands *in front of the house* (instr.).
Byłem *u lekarza.*   I was *at the doctor's* (gen.).

12. Complement of verb of motion

a. Place to which (usually **do** + genitive or **na** + accusative, depending on the type of noun; see Chapter 7)

Ewa idzie *do domu.*   Ewa is going *home* (gen.).
Idę *do dentysty.*   I'm going *to the dentist's* (gen.).
Ewa idzie *na koncert.*   Ewa goes *to a concert* (acc.).

b. Place from which (usually **z** + genitive; with people, **od** + genitive)

Ewa wraca *z pracy.*   Ewa returns *from work* (gen.).
Wracam *od mojego przyjaciela.*   I'm returning *from my friend's* (gen.).

13. Possessor (genitive)

To jest dom *Ewy.*   That is *Ewa's* house.

14. Object of a preposition in a phrase of accompaniment or interaction (**z** + instrumental case)

Idę do kina *z Ewą.*   I'm going to the movies *with Ewa.*
Zawsze kłócę się *z Adamem.*   I always quarrel *with Adam.*

15. Idiomatic phrases (genitive, accusative, or instrumental, according to the expression)

następnego dnia   next day (gen. of time)
całą noc   all night long (acc. of time)
wieczorem   in the evening (instr. of time)

Regular Noun Endings

Here is a summary chart of regular noun endings by gender. In many instances, there is a choice of ending, which is usually determined by the stem consonant (the consonant at the end of the word after the ending is removed). For rules on the distribution of endings, see below. A dash (—) means no ending.

	Feminine	Masculine	Neuter
Singular			
Nom.	-a (-i) | —	—	-o | -e
Gen.	-y/-i	-u | -a	-a
Dat.	-'e | -y/-i	-owi (-u)	-u
Acc.	-ę | —	= Nom. | Gen.	= Nom.
Instr.	-ą	-em	-em
Loc.	= Dat.	-'e | -u	-'e | -u
Voc.	-o | -y/-i	= Loc.	= Nom.
Plural			
Nom./Voc.	-y/-i | -e	-y/-i or -'i | -e	-a
Gen.	— | -y/-i	-ów | -y/-i	— (-y/-i)
Dat.	-om	-om	-om
Acc.	= Nom.	= Nom. | Gen.	= Nom.
Instr.	-ami	-ami	-ami
Loc.	-ach	-ach	-ach

Consonants soften before -'e (dative and locative singular feminine, locative and vocative singular masculine, and locative singular neuter) and before -'i (nominative plural masculine persons). For a chart of softenings and further discussion, see below under Case Forms Involving Hard and Soft Consonants.

When there is a choice among endings in the chart above, use the following rules for the distribution of endings.

Feminine Nouns

1. **Hard stems.** Hard-stem feminine nouns in -a, like **kobieta** *woman,* take endings on the left; soft-stem feminine nouns in —, like **twarz** *face,* take endings on the right; soft-stem feminine nouns in -a (like **ulica** *street*) or in -i (like **gospodyni** *landlady*) take the highlighted alternatives. For charts of full declensions, see below.

2. **Soft stems.** Soft-stem diminutive and affectionate names have a vocative singular in -u: **Basia** *Barb* → voc.sg. **Basiu.**

3. **Dative/locative singular.** Before dative/locative singular -'e, consonants soften: **nodze** (**nog-** + 'e, from **noga** *leg*).

Masculine Nouns

1. **Genitive singular.** Animate nouns have a genitive singular in **-a**. Most inanimate nouns have a genitive singular in **-u**. There are many exceptions and minor rules. For example, the following masculine inanimate nouns have a genitive singular in **-a**: names for tools (**młot** *hammer* → **młota**), card games (**poker** *poker* → **pokera**), dances (**walc** *waltz* → **walca**), months (**listopad** *November* → **listopada**), serially produced food items (**pączek** *doughnut* → **pączka**), and most Polish towns (**Gdańsk** *Gdansk* → **Gdańska**). Important exceptions are **chleb** *bread* → **chleba** and **ser** *cheese* → **sera** (compare **miód** *honey* → **miodu**), and **szpital** *hospital* → **szpitala** (compare **hotel** *hotel* → **hotelu**).

2. **Dative singular.** A small group of masculine nouns have a dative singular in **-u**: **pan** *gentleman* → **panu**, **chłopiec** *boy* → **chłopcu**, **diabeł** *devil* → **diabłu**, **kot** *cat* → **kotu**, **ksiądz** *priest* → **księdzu**, **ojciec** *father* → **ojcu**, **pies** *dog* → **psu**, **świat** *world* → **światu**.

3. **Accusative singular.** Animate nouns have an accusative singular like the genitive singular in **-a**: **pies** *dog* → gen.sg./acc.sg. **psa**. Inanimate nouns have an accusative singular like the nominative singular in —: **zeszyt** *notebook* → nom.sg./acc.sg. **zeszyt**.

4. **Locative/vocative singular.** Velar- and soft-stem nouns have the locative/vocative singular in **-u**: **hotel** *hotel* → **hotelu**, **ręcznik** *towel* → **ręczniku**. Others have the locative/vocative singular in **-'e** and the preceding consonant is softened: **zeszycie** (**zeszyt** + **-'e**, from **zeszyt** *notebook*).

5. **Nominative/vocative plural.** Hard-stem nouns have the nominative/vocative plural in **-y/-i**: **zeszyt** *notebook* → **zeszyty**. Personal nouns soften the stem consonant: **student** *student* → **studenci** (**student** + **-'y/-i**). Soft-stem masculine nouns have **-e**: **kraj** *country* → **kraje**. Titles and relation names tend to have **-owie**: **pan** *sir* → **panowie**, **syn** *son* → **synowie**, **ojciec** *father* → **ojcowie**, **mąż** *husband* → **mężowie**.

6. **Genitive plural.** Hard-stem nouns have the genitive plural in **-ów**: **zeszyt** *notebook* → **zeszytów**. Most soft-stem nouns have **-y/-i**: **hotel** *hotel* → **hoteli**. Some, especially stems in **c**, **dz**, and **j**, have **-ów**: **kraj** *country* → **krajów**. All nouns with the nominative plural in **-owie** *have* **-ów**: **mąż** *husband* → **mężowie, mężów**.

7. **Accusative plural.** Personal nouns have the accusative plural like the genitive plural: **student** *student* → **studentów**. All others have the accusative plural like the nominative plural: **hotel** *hotel* → **hotele**, **zeszyt** *notebook* → **zeszyty**.

Neuter Nouns

1. **Nominative/accusative/vocative singular.** Hard-stem neuter nouns have the nominative/accusative/vocative singular in **-o**: **drzewo** *tree*. Soft-stem neuter nouns have **-e**: **pole** *field,* **pytanie** *question.*

2. **Locative singular.** Velar- and soft-stem nouns have the locative singular in **-u**: **pole** *field* → **polu, łóżko** *bed* → **łóżku**. Others have **-'e** and the preceding consonant is softened: **biuro** *office* → **biurze (biur-'e)**.

3. **Nominative/accusative/vocative plural.** Neuter nouns have the nominative/accusative/vocative plural in **-a**: **drzewo** *tree* → **drzewa, mieszkanie** *apartment* → **mieszkania, zwierzę** *animal* → **zwierzęta, imię** *name* → **imiona, muzeum** *museum* → **muzea**. Exceptions are **dziecko** *child* → **dzieci, oko** *eye* → **oczy**, and **ucho** *ear* → **uszy**.

4. **Genitive plural in -y/-i.** Some soft-stem neuter nouns that have a collective meaning or that name areas or spaces, have the genitive plural in **-y/-i**: **wybrzeże** *seacoast* → **wybrzeży, narzędzie** *tool* → **narzędzi**.

5. **Genitive plural in -ów.** A very few neuters, most importantly those in **-um**, do not decline in the singular; they have the genitive plural in **-ów** (see the declension of **muzeum** below).

6. **Nominative/accusative/vocative singular in -ę.** A few neuter nouns have the nominative/accusative/vocative singular in **-ę** and have soft stems in the singular, but hard stems in the plural: **imię** *name* → **imienia**, pl. **imiona, zwierzę** *animal* → **zwierzęcia**, pl. **zwierzęta**.

Case Forms Involving Hard and Soft Consonants

The noun endings that take the most time to learn are those that depend on whether the stem consonant (the consonant before the nominative singular ending) is hard or soft. Endings that depend on this distinction are (a) the locative singular of all nouns, (b) the dative singular of feminine nouns (which is identical to the locative), (c) the nominative/accusative plural of masculine and feminine nouns, including masculine personal nouns, and (d) the genitive plural of masculine nouns. Much of the following information is a reorganization of material presented above.

Here is a chart of Polish hard ("plain") consonants and their corresponding soft consonants:

Hard	p	b	f	w	m	t	d	s	z	n	ł
Soft	p'	b'	f'	w'	m'	ć	dź	ś	ź	ń	l

Hard	r	k	g	ch	st	zd	sł	zł	sn		
Soft	rz	c	dz	sz/ś	ść	źdź	śl	źl	śń	cz	ż	j

Locative Singular

Here is the short description for forming the locative singular (and the dative singular of feminine nouns): Hard-stem nouns have **-e** and the stem consonant is softened, while soft-stem nouns have the other ending (see the noun endings chart above), which for feminine nouns is **-y/-i** and for masculine and neuter nouns is **-u**. For feminine nouns, stem-ending **k**, **g**, and **ch** are softenable, whereas for masculine and neuter nouns, they are not; hence, they take the other ending, **-u**. Here are the details:

1. **Feminine nouns.** Feminine nouns form the locative/dative singular by adding **-e** to a hard (that is, softenable) stem consonant, including **k**, **g**, and **ch**, and softening the consonant: **kobieta** *woman* → **kobiecie**, **książka** *book* → **książce**. Non-softenable consonants have **-y (-i)**: **ulica** *street* → **ulicy**, **rzecz** *thing* → **rzeczy**, **kość** *bone* → **kości**. In the feminine locative, stem-ending **ch** becomes **sz**: **mucha** *fly* → **musze**.

2. **Masculine and neuter nouns.** Masculine and neuter nouns form the locative singular by adding **-e** to a softenable stem consonant and softening the consonant. Remember that sounds like **p'** and **ć** are spelled **pi-** and **ci-**, respectively: **zeszyt** *notebook* → **zeszycie**. Non-softenable consonants, including **k**, **g**, and **ch**, have **-u**: **hotel** *hotel* → **hotelu**, **mieszkanie** *apartment* → **mieszkaniu**, **ręcznik** *towel* → **ręczniku**, **pudełko** *box* → **pudełku**. Irregular locatives include **dom** *house* → **domu**, **pan** *sir* → **panu**, and **syn** *son* → **synu**.

Notes

Before the ending **-'e** (**-e** plus softening of the preceding consonant), most nouns with **-ia-** or **-io-/-ió-** in the root before **t**, **d**, **s**, or **z**, change the **-ia-** or **-io-/-ió-** to **-ie-** in the locative singular: **sąsiad** *neighbor* → **sąsiedzie**, **kościół** *church* → **kościele**. The potential change of root **ą** to **ę** and **ó** to **o** in masculine nouns before all endings applies here too: **mąż** *husband* → **mężu**, **stół** *table* → **stole**. Mobile **e**, which occurs in many masculine noun stems, is dropped before all endings: **budynek** *building* → loc.sg. **budynku**.

Nominative Plural

Here is the short description for forming the nominative plural of nouns: Neuter nouns have **-a**, hard-stem masculine and feminine nouns have **-y/-i**, and soft-stem masculine and feminine nouns have **-e**. In masculine personal nouns, the stem consonant softens before **-y/-i**. Here are the details:

1. **Neuter nouns.** Neuter nouns form the nominative/accusative/vocative plural by adding **-a**: **drzewo** *tree* → **drzewa**, **mieszkanie** *apartment* → **mieszkania**, **muzeum** *museum* → **muzea**. Special forms are **imię** *name* → **imiona** and **zwierzę** *animal* → **zwierzęta**. Exceptions are **dziecko** *child* → **dzieci**, **oko** *eye* → **oczy**, and **ucho** *ear* → **uszy**.

2. **Masculine non-personal nouns and feminine nouns.** Masculine non-personal nouns and all feminine nouns (personal or otherwise) usually form the nominative/accusative/vocative plural by adding **-y/-i** to hard consonants (**-i** is used after **k** and **g**) and **-e** to soft consonants: **zeszyt** *notebook* → **zeszyty, ołówek** *pencil* → **ołówki, hotel** *hotel* → **hotele, dziewczyna** *girl* → **dziewczyny, książka** *book* → **książki, ulica** *street* → **ulice.** Feminine nouns that do not end in **-a** have either **-y/-i** or **-e** in the nominative/accusative/vocative plural: **rzecz** *thing* → **rzeczy, powieść** *novel* → **powieści, twarz** *face* → **twarze.**

3. **Masculine personal nouns.** Masculine personal nouns form the nominative/accusative/vocative plural by adding **-y/-i**, as expected, but the stem consonant is softened before this ending. In the masculine personal plural, both **ch** and **sz** become **ś** (or **s** before **-i**): **Czech** *Czech* → **Czesi, starszy asystent** *senior assistant* → **starsi asystenci.** Many masculine personal nouns, especially names for relations, have **-owie: pan** *gentleman* → **pano-wie, ojciec** *father* → **ojcowie, syn** *son* → **synowie.** Irregular nominative/accusative/vocative plural forms are **brat** *brother* → **bracia** and **człowiek** *man, human* → **ludzie.** A few ethnic names have **-'e: Amerykanin** *American* → **Amerykanie, Cygan** *Gypsy* → **Cyganie.**

Genitive Plural

Here is the short description for forming the genitive plural of nouns: If the nominative singular ends in a vowel (**-a, -o, -e**), the genitive plural ending is **—**. Otherwise, the ending is **-ów** for hard-stem nouns and **-y/-i** for soft-stem nouns. Here are the details:

1. **Feminine and neuter nouns.** The genitive plural of feminine and neuter nouns is usually **—**, that is, there is no ending at all: **kobieta** *woman* → **kobiet, drzewo** *tree* → **drzew.** Often, the change of root **ę** to **ą** and **o** to **ó** takes place: **wstęga** *ribbon* → **wstąg, pole** *field* → **pól.** Mobile **e** often breaks up the final two stem consonants: **wiosna** *spring* → **wiosen, wiadro** *bucket* → **wiader.** This almost always happens before **k: książka** *book* → **książek, łóżko** *bed* → **łóżek.** In a few exceptional instances, the ending **-y/-i** occurs instead of **—: wybrzeże** *seacoast* → **wybrzeży, skrzela** *gill* → **skrzeli.**

2. **Masculine nouns.** The genitive plural of masculine nouns is usually **-ów** for hard-stem nouns and **-y/-i** for soft-stem nouns: **student** *student* → **stu-dentów, hotel** *hotel* → **hoteli.** However, many nouns with stems in **dz, c,** and **j**, and a few other nouns, have **-ów** instead of the expected **-y/-i: kraj** *country* → **krajów, cel** *goal, aim* → **celów.** A masculine personal noun with the nominative plural in **-owie** has the genitive/accusative plural in **-ów**, no matter what the stem is: **sędzia** *judge* (pl. **sędziowie**) → **sędziów.** Note that

with masculine personal nouns, the genitive plural form is also used for the accusative plural: **Widzę tych studentów.** *I see those students.*

Charts of Representative Noun Declensions

Here are the full declensions of representative Polish nouns of all three genders. Remember the following points:

1. For masculine animate nouns, the accusative singular is like the genitive singular; for inanimate nouns, the accusative singular is like the nominative singular. For masculine personal nouns, the accusative plural is like the genitive plural. For all feminine, neuter, and masculine non-personal nouns, the accusative plural is like the nominative plural.

2. Neuter nouns have identical nominative and accusative forms in both the singular and plural.

3. Feminine nouns have identical dative and locative forms in the singular, and identical nominative and accusative forms in the plural.

4. With rare exceptions, nouns have the same dative, instrumental, and locative forms in the plural (**-om**, **-ami**, **-ach**, respectively), regardless of gender.

5. The vocative plural of all nouns is like the nominative plural.

Masculine Nouns

Masculine Non-Personal Nouns

	Singular	Plural	Singular	Plural
	sklep *store* (hard stem)		**hotel** *hotel* (soft stem)	
Nom.	sklep	sklepy	hotel	hotele
Gen.	sklepu	sklepów	hotelu	hoteli
Dat.	sklepowi	sklepom	hotelowi	hotelom
Acc.	sklep	sklepy	hotel	hotele
Instr.	sklepem	sklepami	hotelem	hotelami
Loc.	sklepie	sklepach	hotelu	hotelach
Voc.	sklepie	sklepy	hotelu	hotele
	stół *table* (hard stem, ó → o)		**gołąb** *pigeon* (animate, soft labial stem)	
Nom.	stół	stoły	gołąb	gołębie
Gen.	stołu	stołów	gołębia	gołębi
Dat.	stołowi	stołom	gołębiowi	gołębiom
Acc.	stół	stoły	gołębia	gołębie
Instr.	stołem	stołami	gołębiem	gołębiami
Loc.	stole	stołach	gołębiu	gołębiach
Voc.	stole	stoły	gołębiu	gołębie

	Singular	Plural		Singular	Plural
	pies *dog* (animate, mobile **e**, dat.sg. in **-u**)			**kot** *cat* (animate, dat.sg. in **-u**)	
Nom.	pies	psy		kot	koty
Gen.	psa	psów		kota	kotów
Dat.	psu	psom		kotu	kotom
Acc.	psa	psy		kota	koty
Instr.	psem	psami		kotem	kotami
Loc.	psie	psach		kocie	kotach
Voc.	psie	psy		kocie	koty
	dzień *day* (soft stem, mobile **e**)			**tydzień** *week* (soft stem, irreg. stem)	
Nom.	dzień	dni(e)		tydzień	tygodnie
Gen.	dnia	dni		tygodnia	tygodni
Dat.	dniowi	dniom		tygodniowi	tygodniom
Acc.	dzień	dni(e)		tydzień	tygodnie
Instr.	dniem	dniami		tygodniem	tygodniami
Loc.	dniu	dniach		tygodniu	tygodniach
Voc.	dniu	dni(e)		tygodniu	tygodnie
	rok *year* (exceptional pl.)			**miesiąc** *month* (irreg. gen.pl.)	
Nom.	rok	lata		miesiąc	miesiące
Gen.	roku	lat		miesiąca	miesięcy
Dat.	rokowi	latom		miesiącowi	miesiącom
Acc.	rok	lata		miesiąc	miesiące
Instr.	rokiem	laty (latami)		miesiącem	miesiącami
Loc.	roku	latach		miesiącu	miesiącach
Voc.	roku	lata		miesiącu	miesiące

Masculine Personal Nouns

	Singular	Plural	Singular	Plural
	student *student*		**lekarz** *doctor* (soft stem)	
Nom.	student	studenci	lekarz	lekarze
Gen.	studenta	studentów	lekarza	lekarzy
Dat.	studentowi	studentom	lekarzowi	lekarzom
Acc.	studenta	studentów	lekarza	lekarzy
Instr.	studentem	studentami	lekarzem	lekarzami
Loc.	studencie	studentach	lekarzu	lekarzach
Voc.	studencie	studenci	lekarzu	lekarze
	brat *brother* (special pl.)		**mąż** *husband*	
Nom.	brat	bracia	mąż	mężowie
Gen.	brata	braci	męża	mężów
Dat.	bratu	braciom	mężowi	mężom
Acc.	brata	braci	męża	mężów
Instr.	bratem	braćmi	mężem	mężami
Loc.	bracie	braciach	mężu	mężach
Voc.	bracie	bracia	mężu	mężowie
	przyjaciel *friend* (special pl.)		**syn** *son* (special loc. and pl.)	
Nom.	przyjaciel	przyjaciele	syn	synowie
Gen.	przyjaciela	przyjaciół	syna	synów
Dat.	przyjacielowi	przyjaciołom	synowi	synom
Acc.	przyjaciela	przyjaciół	syna	synów
Instr.	przyjacielem	przyjaciółmi	synem	synami
Loc.	przyjacielu	przyjaciołach	synu	synach
Voc.	przyjacielu	przyjaciele	synu	synowie
	człowiek *man* (suppletive pl.)		**ojciec** *father* (irreg. stem, irreg. dat./voc.sg.)	
Nom.	człowiek	ludzie	ojciec	ojcowie
Gen.	człowieka	ludzi	ojca	ojców
Dat.	człowiekowi	ludziom	ojcu	ojcom
Acc.	człowieka	ludzi	ojca	ojców
Instr.	człowiekiem	ludźmi	ojcem	ojcami
Loc.	człowieku	ludziach	ojcu	ojcach
Voc.	człowieku	ludzie	ojcze	ojcowie

Feminine Nouns

	Singular	Plural
	kobieta *woman* (hard stem)	
Nom.	kobieta	kobiety
Gen.	kobiety	kobiet
Dat.	kobiecie	kobietom
Acc.	kobietę	kobiety
Instr.	kobietą	kobietami
Loc.	kobiecie	kobietach
Voc.	kobieto	kobiety

	Singular	Plural
	ulica *street* (soft stem)	
Nom.	ulica	ulice
Gen.	ulicy	ulic
Dat.	ulicy	ulicom
Acc.	ulicę	ulice
Instr.	ulicą	ulicami
Loc.	ulicy	ulicach
Voc.	ulico	ulice

	noga *leg, foot* (velar stem)	
Nom.	noga	nogi
Gen.	nogi	nóg
Dat.	nodze	nogom
Acc.	nogę	nogi
Instr.	nogą	nogami
Loc.	nodze	nogach
Voc.	nogo	nogi

	ręka *hand, arm* (velar stem, irreg. pl.)	
Nom.	ręka	ręce
Gen.	ręki	rąk
Dat.	ręce	rękom
Acc.	rękę	ręce
Instr.	ręką	rękami
Loc.	ręce (ręku)	rękach
Voc.	ręko	ręce

	rzeka *river* (velar stem)	
Nom.	rzeka	rzeki
Gen.	rzeki	rzek
Dat.	rzece	rzekom
Acc.	rzekę	rzeki
Instr.	rzeką	rzekami
Loc.	rzece	rzekach
Voc.	rzeko	rzeki

	noc *night* (nom.sg. in —)	
Nom.	noc	noce
Gen.	nocy	nocy
Dat.	nocy	nocom
Acc.	noc	noce
Instr.	nocą	nocami
Loc.	nocy	nocach
Voc.	nocy	noce

	kość *bone* (nom.sg. in —)	
Nom.	kość	kości
Gen.	kości	kości
Dat.	kości	kościom
Acc.	kość	kości
Instr.	kością	kościami (kośćmi)
Loc.	kości	kościach
Voc.	kości	kości

	gospodyni *landlady* (nom.sg. in -i)	
Nom.	gospodyni	gospodynie
Gen.	gospodyni	gospodyń
Dat.	gospodyni	gospodyniom
Acc.	gospodynię	gospodynie
Instr.	gospodynią	gospodyniami
Loc.	gospodyni	gospodyniach
Voc.	gospodyni	gospodynie

Neuter Nouns

	Singular	Plural	Singular	Plural
	miasto *town* (hard stem)		**zdanie** *opinion* (soft stem)	
Nom.-Voc.	miasto	miasta	zdanie	zdania
Gen.	miasta	miast	zdania	zdań
Dat.	miastu	miastom	zdaniu	zdaniom
Acc.	miasto	miasta	zdanie	zdania
Instr.	miastem	miastami	zdaniem	zdaniami
Loc.	mieście	miastach	zdaniu	zdaniach
	oko *eye* (unique pl.)		**ucho** *ear* (unique pl.)	
Nom.-Voc.	oko	oczy	ucho	uszy
Gen.	oka	oczu	ucha	uszu
Dat.	oku	oczom	uchu	uszom
Acc.	oko	oczy	ucho	uszy
Instr.	okiem	oczami	uchem	uszami
Loc.	oku	oczach	uchu	uszach
	muzeum *museum* (-um type)		**dziecko** *child* (unique pl.)	
Nom.-Voc.	muzeum	muzea	dziecko	dzieci
Gen.	muzeum	muzeów	dziecka	dzieci
Dat.	muzeum	muzeom	dziecku	dzieciom
Acc.	muzeum	muzea	dziecko	dzieci
Instr.	muzeum	muzeami	dzieckiem	dziećmi
Loc.	muzeum	muzeach	dziecku	dzieciach
	zwierzę *animal* (-ę/-ęcia type)		**imię** *first name* (-ę/-enia type)	
Nom.-Voc.	zwierzę	zwierzęta	imię	imiona
Gen.	zwierzęcia	zwierząt	imienia	imion
Dat.	zwierzęciu	zwierzętom	imieniu	imionom
Acc.	zwierzę	zwierzęta	imię	imiona
Instr.	zwierzęciem	zwierzętami	imieniem	imionami
Loc.	zwierzęciu	zwierzętach	imieniu	imionach

Supplements

Days of the Week

poniedziałek	Monday	w poniedziałek	on Monday
wtorek	Tuesday	we wtorek	on Tuesday
środa	Wednesday	w środę	on Wednesday
czwartek	Thursday	w czwartek	on Thursday
piątek	Friday	w piątek	on Friday
sobota	Saturday	w sobotę	on Saturday
niedziela	Sunday	w niedzielę	on Sunday

Compass Directions

północ	north	na północy	in the north
południe	south	na południu	in the south
wschód	east	na wschodzie	in the east
zachód	west	na zachodzie	in the west

Months

styczeń	January	w styczniu	in January
luty	February	w lutym	in February
marzec	March	w marcu	in March
kwiecień	April	w kwietniu	in April
maj	May	w maju	in May
czerwiec	June	w czerwcu	in June
lipiec	July	w lipcu	in July
sierpień	August	w sierpniu	in August
wrzesień	September	we wrześniu	in September
październik	October	w październiku	in October
listopad	November	w listopadzie	in November
grudzień	December	w grudniu	in December

Irregular Country Names

Most Polish names for countries are regular and are declined like other nouns. The following exceptions are plural in form and belong to an archaic declension.

Country	Polish Name	"In the Country"	"To the Country"
China	Chiny	w Chinach	do Chin
Czech Republic	Czechy	w Czechach	do Czech
Germany	Niemcy	w Niemczech	do Niemiec
Hungary	Węgry	na Węgrzech	na Węgry
Italy	Włochy	we Włoszech	do Włoch

Common First Names and Their Diminutives

Polish first names (typically, the names of Roman Catholic saints) usually have, in addition to the formal variant of the name, a diminutive, or informal, variant, used among friends. Often, a diminutive of the second degree also exists, used affectionately, especially among intimates and with children.

Male

Adam, Adaś, Adi
Aleksander, Aleks, Olek
Andrzej, Jędrek, Jędruś, Andrzejek
Bogdan, Bogdanek, Boguś, Bodek
Bogusław, Boguś, Sławek
Bolesław, Bolek, Boluś
Bronisław, Bronek
Czesław, Czesiek, Czesio
Daniel, Danielek
Dariusz, Darek, Daruś, Dareczek
Edward, Edek, Edzio, Edi
Emil, Emilek, Milek, Miluś, Emi
Eugeniusz, Gienek, Geniuś, Gienio, Genek
Feliks, Felek, Feluś
Filip, Filek, Filipek, Filuś, Fifi
Franciszek, Franek, Franuś, Franio
Fryderyk, Frydek, Fryc, Frycek
Grzegorz, Grzesiek, Grzesio, Grześ, Grzesiu
Henryk, Heniek, Henio, Heniuś
Ignacy, Ignacek, Ignaś
Ireneusz, Irek, Iruś
Jacek, Jacuś
Jakub, Kuba, Jakubek, Kubuś
Jan, Janek, Jasiek, Jasio, Jaś
Janusz, Januszek, Janek, Janeczek
Jarosław, Jarek
Jerzy, Jurek, Jureczek
Józef, Józek, Józeczek, Józio, Józuś
Julian, Julianek
Juliusz, Julek
Kamil, Kamilek
Karol, Karolek, Lolek
Kazimierz, Kazik, Kazio, Kazek
Konrad, Konradek, Radek
Konstanty, Kostek, Kostuś
Krzysztof, Krzysiek, Krzyś
Lech, Leszek, Lesio, Lesiu

Lucjan, Lucek
Ludwik, Ludek
Łukasz, Łukaszek
Maciej, Maciek, Maciuś
Marcin, Marcinek
Marek, Mareczek, Maruś
Marian, Marianek, Maryś, Mariuś, Maniek, Manio
Mariusz, Mariuszek, Mariuś
Mateusz, Mateuszek, Mati
Michał, Michałek, Michaś, Misiek
Mieczysław, Mietek, Miecio
Mikołaj, Mikołajek
Miron, Mirek
Mirosław, Mirek
Olaf, Olek, Olo
Oskar, Oskarek
Paweł, Pawełek
Piotr, Piotrek, Piotruś
Rafał, Rafałek, Rafcio
Robert, Robuś, Robek, Robcio, Bercik
Roman, Romek, Romeczek, Romuś, Romcio
Ryszard, Rysiek, Rysio, Ryś
Sławomir, Sławek, Sławuś, Sławcio
Stanisław, Stasiek, Stasio, Staś, Stacho, Staszek
Stefan, Stefek, Stefanek, Stefcio
Szymon, Szymek, Szymuś
Tadeusz, Tadek, Tadzio, Tadeuszek, Tadzik
Tomasz, Tomek, Tomuś, Tomcio
Wacław, Wacek, Wacuś
Waldemar, Waldek, Walduś, Waldzio
Walery, Walerek
Wiesław, Wiesiek, Wiesio
Wiktor, Wiktorek
Wincenty, Wicek, Wicuś
Witold, Witek, Wituś, Wicio
Władysław, Władek, Władzio
Włodzimierz, Włodek, Włodzio
Wojciech, Wojtek, Wojtuś
Zbigniew, Zbyszek, Zbynio, Zbysio, Zbych, Zbysiek
Zdzisław, Zdzisiek, Zdziś
Zenon, Zenek, Zenuś
Zygmunt, Zygmuś, Zygmuntek, Zyguś

Female

Agata, Agatka, Aga, Agusia
Agnieszka, Agunia, Agusia, Aga, Jagna, Jagienka

Aleksandra, Ola, Ala, Oleńka, Olka
Alicja, Ala, Alusia, Alka
Alina, Ala, Alusia, Alka, Alinka
Aneta, Anetka
Aniela, Anielka
Anna, Ania, Anka, Hanka
Barbara, Basia, Baśka
Beata, Beatka
Bogdana, Bogdanka
Bogumiła, Bogusia, Miłka
Bogusława, Bogusia, Boguśka, Gusia
Bożena, Bożenka, Bożusia
Cecylia, Cyla, Cylka, Cesia
Danuta, Danusia, Danka
Dominika, Domiczka, Dominiczka, Nika, Domi
Dorota, Dora, Dorotka, Dorocia
Edyta, Edytka, Edzia
Elżbieta, Ela, Elunia, Elka, Elza, Elżbietka
Emilia, Emilka, Emi
Ewa, Ewunia, Ewcia, Ewusia, Ewka
Felicja, Fela, Felka
Gabriela, Gabrysia, Gabryśka, Gabusia, Gabi
Grażyna, Grażynka, Graża, Grażka
Halina, Hala, Halka, Halusia, Halinka
Hanna, Hania, Hanusia, Hanka
Hedwiga, Hedzia, Hedwisia
Helena, Hela, Helenka, Helcia
Henryka, Henia, Heńka
Irena, Irenka, Ircia, Irusia, Irka
Iwona, Iwonka, Iwa, Iwka, Iwcia
Izabela, Iza, Izunia, Izka, Bella
Jadwiga, Jadzia, Jaga, Jadźka, Jadwisia
Janina, Janka, Janinka, Janeczka
Joanna, Joasia, Aśka
Jolanta, Jola, Jolusia, Jolcia, Jolka
Józefa, Józia, Józka, Ziuta
Judyta, Judytka, Judysia
Julia, Jula, Julcia, Julka
Justyna, Justynka, Justysia, Justa
Karolina, Karolcia, Karolinka, Karolka, Lola
Katarzyna, Kasia, Kasieńka, Kaśka, Kasiunia, Katarzynka
Kazimiera, Kazia
Klara, Klarusia, Klarcia
Klaudia, Klaudisia, Klaudyna
Krystyna, Krysia, Kryśka, Krystynka
Leokadia, Lodzia, Loda, Leosia

Lidia, Lidka, Lidzia
Liliana, Lila, Lilcia, Lilka, Lilianka
Lucyna, Luca, Lucusia, Lusia, Lucynka, Lucia
Ludwika, Lusia, Ludka, Ludzia
Magdalena, Magda, Madzia, Magdusia, Magdalenka
Maja, Majka, Majeczka
Małgorzata, Małgosia, Gosia, Małgośka, Gośka
Maria, Marysia, Maryś, Marynia
Mariola, Mariolka
Marta, Marcia, Martunia, Martusia
Maryla, Marylka
Marzena, Marzenka
Mirosława, Mirka, Mirusia, Mira
Monika, Moniczka, Monisia, Misia, Nika, Monia, Mona
Natalia, Tala, Natalka, Natka, Nati
Olga, Ola, Oleńka, Olka, Olgusia
Oliwia, Oliwka, Ola
Patrycja, Pati, Patka
Paulina, Paulinka, Paula
Regina, Reginka, Rena
Renata, Renia, Renatka
Róża, Rózia, Różyczka
Stanisława, Stasia, Staśka
Stefania, Stefa, Stefcia, Stefka
Sylwia, Sylwiunia, Sylwka, Sylwcia
Teresa, Teresia, Renia, Terenia, Tereska
Urszula, Ula, Urszulka, Ulka, Usia
Wanda, Wandzia
Weronika, Weroniczka, Weronka, Wera, Werka, Nika
Wiesława, Wiesia, Wieśka
Wiktoria, Wika, Wiktorka, Wiki
Zofia, Zosia, Zosieńka, Zośka

3. Pronouns

Personal Pronouns

Singular		Plural		Other	
ja	I	**my**	we	**co**	what
ty	you (*sg.*)	**wy**	you (*pl.*)	**nic**	nothing
on	he	**oni**	they (*masc.pers.*)	**kto**	who
ona	she	**one**	they (*non-masc.pers.*)	**nikt**	no one
ono	it				

The pronoun **oni** is used for both all-male and mixed male and female groups; **one** is used for groups that have no male persons. Personal pronouns, especially first- and second-person pronouns, are normally not used as the subjects of verbs except for emphasis; hence, one usually says **robię** *I do* instead of **ja robię** *I do.* The pronoun **kto** is considered masculine for purposes of agreement, even when it refers to a group of women: **Kto jest głodny?** *Who is hungry?* The pronouns **nic** and **nikt** are used with a negated verb.

Nic nie rozumiem.	I don't understand anything.
Nikt tu nie mieszka.	No one lives here.

Pronouns of Polite, Formal Address

Singular		Plural	
pan	sir, you, Mr.	**panowie**	sirs, you (*masc.pers.pl.*)
pani	madam, you, Mrs., Miss, Ms.	**panie**	madams, you (*fem.pl.*)
		państwo	ladies and gentlemen, you, Mr. and Mrs.

The title **państwo** looks like a singular form, but it is considered masculine personal plural for purposes of verb and adjective agreement. It refers to a group of male and female persons individually referred to as **pan** and **pani**, and it also refers to a married couple, as in **państwo Zielińscy** *Mr. and Mrs. Zieliński.*

The pronouns of polite, formal address show respect and distance. They are used to address a stranger, a person one does not know well, or a person of authority or status. The informal **ty** *you* and its plural, **wy**, convey friendliness, closeness, and familiarity. They are used to address family members, close friends, and pets. Their use with strangers or superiors is apt to sound rude. For more information on the use of pronouns, see Chapter 9.

Personal pronouns show a full range of case forms, summarized in the following charts.

Interrogative and Negative Pronouns

Nom.	**co** *what*	**nic** *nothing*	**kto** *who*	**nikt** *no one*
Gen.	**czego**	**niczego, nic**	**kogo**	**nikogo**
Dat.	**czemu**	**niczemu**	**komu**	**nikomu**
Acc.	**co**	**nic**	**kogo**	**nikogo**
Instr.	**czym**	**niczym**	**kim**	**nikim**
Loc.	**czym**	**niczym**	**kim**	**nikim**

First- and Second-Person Pronouns

Nom.	**ja** *I*	**ty** *you* (sg.)	**my** *we*	**wy** *you* (pl.)
Gen.	**mnie**	**cię, ciebie**	**nas**	**was**
Dat.	**mi, mnie**	**ci, tobie**	**nam**	**wam**
Acc.	**mnie**	**cię, ciebie**	**nas**	**was**
Instr.	**mną**	**tobą**	**nami**	**wami**
Loc.	**mnie**	**tobie**	**nas**	**was**

The longer forms **mnie**, **ciebie**, and **tobie** are emphatic; they are also automatically used after prepositions. Accusative **mnie** is often pronounced, but rarely spelled, **mię**.

Third-Person Singular Pronouns

Nom.	**on** *he, it*	**ona** *she, it*	**ono** *it*
Gen.	**go, jego, niego**	**jej, niej**	**go, jego, niego**
Dat.	**mu, jemu, niemu**	**jej, niej**	**mu, jemu, niemu**
Acc.	**go, jego, niego**	**ją, nią**	**je, nie**
Instr.	**nim**	**nią**	**nim**
Loc.	**nim**	**niej**	**nim**

The longer form **jego** is emphatic; it is also automatically used after prepositions. After a preposition, forms beginning in **i-** or **j-** lose the **i-** or **j-** and substitute **ni-** instead: **dla + ich → dla nich** *to them*, **bez + jej → bez niej** *without her*.

Third-Person Plural Pronouns

Nom.	**oni** *they* (masc.pers.)	**one** *they* (other)
Gen.	**ich, nich**	**ich, nich**
Dat.	**im, nim**	**im, nim**
Acc.	**ich, nich**	**je, nie**
Instr.	**nimi**	**nimi**
Loc.	**nich**	**nich**

Third-Person Pronouns of Formal Address

Nom.	**pan** *you* (masc.)	**panowie** (pl. of **pan**)	**państwo** *you* (masc.pers.pl.)
Gen.	**pana**	**panów**	**państwa**
Dat.	**panu**	**panom**	**państwu**
Acc.	**pana**	**panów**	**państwa**
Instr.	**panem**	**panami**	**państwem**
Loc.	**panu**	**panach**	**państwu**
Voc.	**panie**	**panowie**	**państwo**
Nom.	**pani** *you* (fem.)	**panie** (pl. of **pani**)	**państwo** *you*
Gen.	**pani**	**pań**	(addresses a group
Dat.	**pani**	**paniom**	of both male and
Acc.	**panią**	**panie**	female persons
Instr.	**panią**	**paniami**	referred to
Loc.	**pani**	**paniach**	individually as
Voc.	**pani**	**panie**	**pan** and **pani**)

Reflexive Pronouns

Nom.	—
Gen.	**siebie, się**
Dat.	**sobie, se**
Acc.	**siebie, się**
Instr.	**sobą**
Loc.	**sobie**

The dative reflexive form **se** is restricted to highly informal speech.

Possessive Pronouns

The possessive pronouns **mój moja moje** *my/mine,* **twój twoja twoje** *your/ yours* (sg.), **nasz nasza nasze** *our/ours,* and **wasz wasza wasze** *your/yours* (pl.) have complete declensions in terms of gender, case, and number, in contrast to the genitive-only forms **jego** *his, its,* **jej** *her/hers,* and **ich** *their/ theirs.* The possessive of **pan** *you* (*masc.pers. formal*) is indeclinable **pana** (or, more formally, declinable **pański**), and the possessive of **pani** *your* (*fem. formal*) is **pani**. The reflexive possessive pronoun **swój swoje swoja** *one's own,* with endings like **mój**, is used instead of the other possessive pronouns to modify a noun in the complement of a sentence when the pos- sessor is also the subject of the sentence: **On idzie ze swoją narzeczoną.** *He is coming with his fiancée.* The possessive pronoun **swój swoje swoja** is not used to modify the subject of a sentence, nor is it used after the verb **być** *be.*

mój moja moje *my, mine*

	Masc.	Fem.	Neut.	Masc.Pers.Pl.	Other Pl.
Nom.	mój	moja	moje	moi	moje
Gen.	mojego	mojej	mojego	moich	moich
Dat.	mojemu	mojej	mojemu	moim	moim
Acc.	= Nom./Gen.	moją	= Nom.	= Gen.	= Nom.
Instr.	moim	moją	moim	moimi	moimi
Loc.	moim	mojej	moim	moich	moich

The possessive pronouns **twój twoja twoje** and **swój swoja swoje** are declined like **mój moja moje**.

nasz nasza nasze *our, ours*

	Masc.	Fem.	Neut.	Masc.Pers.Pl.	Other Pl.
Nom.	nasz	nasza	nasze	nasi	nasze
Gen.	naszego	naszej	naszego	naszych	naszych
Dat.	naszemu	naszej	naszemu	naszym	naszym
Acc.	= Nom./Gen.	naszą	= Nom.	= Gen.	= Nom.
Instr.	naszym	naszą	naszym	naszymi	naszymi
Loc.	naszym	naszej	naszym	naszych	naszych

The possessive pronoun **wasz wasza wasze** *your/yours* (pl.) is declined like **nasz nasza nasze**.

Demonstrative and Relative Pronouns

Polish has no indefinite and definite articles analogous to English *a/an* and *the*. Context indicates whether a noun is definite or indefinite. Thus, **stół** may mean either *a table* or *the table*. Often, placement of a noun in a sentence indicates whether it is definite (initial position) or indefinite (final position); compare **Stół stoi w kącie.** *The table stands in the corner.* and **W kącie stoi stół.** *In the corner stands a table.* Definiteness may be emphasized by using the demonstrative pronoun **ten ta to** *this, that*. Both demonstrative and relative pronouns have complete declensions in terms of gender, case, and number.

ten ta to *this, that* (demonstrative pronoun)

	Masc.	Fem.	Neut.	Masc.Pers.Pl.	Other Pl.
Nom.	ten	ta	to	ci	te
Gen.	tego	tej	tego	tych	tych
Dat.	temu	tej	temu	tym	tym
Acc.	= Nom./Gen.	tę	= Nom.	= Gen.	= Nom.
Instr.	tym	tą	tym	tymi	tymi
Loc.	tym	tej	tym	tych	tych

The final ę of tę is not denasalized. Colloquially, tę is often pronounced like tą.

który która które *which, who* (relative and interrogative pronoun)

	Masc.	Fem.	Neut.	Masc.Pers.Pl.	Other Pl.
Nom.	który	która	które	którzy	które
Gen.	którego	której	którego	których	których
Dat.	któremu	której	któremu	którym	którym
Acc.	= Nom./Gen.	którą	= Nom.	= Gen.	= Nom.
Instr.	którym	którą	którym	którymi	którymi
Loc.	którym	której	którym	których	których

jaki jaka jakie *what, what kind* (relative and interrogative pronoun)

	Masc.	Fem.	Neut.	Masc.Pers.Pl.	Other Pl.
Nom.	jaki	jaka	jakie	jacy	jakie
Gen.	jakiego	jakiej	jakiego	jakich	jakich
Dat.	jakiemu	jakiej	jakiemu	jakim	jakim
Acc.	= Nom./Gen.	jaką	= Nom.	= Gen.	= Nom.
Instr.	jakim	jaką	jakim	jakimi	jakimi
Loc.	jakim	jakiej	jakim	jakich	jakich

The difference between **który która które** and **jaki jaka jakie** as an interrogative pronoun is one of specificity: **Który film chcesz obejrzeć?** *Which movie do you want to see?* asks which movie out of a limited number, while **Jaki film chcesz obejrzeć?** *What kind of film do you want to see?* does not limit the range of possible films.

Intensive Pronouns

sam sama samo *self, same, very*

	Masc.	Fem.	Neut.	Masc.Pers.Pl.	Other Pl.
Nom.	sam	sama	samo	sami	same
Gen.	samego	samej	samego	samych	samych
Dat.	samemu	samej	samemu	samym	samym
Acc.	= Nom./Gen.	samą	= Nom.	= Gen.	= Nom.
Instr.	samym	samą	samym	samymi	samymi
Loc.	samym	samej	samym	samych	samych

The intensive pronoun is used in expressions like the following:

Czy robisz to sam?	Are you doing that yourself?
Czy mieszkasz sama?	Do you live alone?
To jest ten sam człowiek.	That is the same man.
Czy mieszkasz w tym samym domu?	Do you live in the same house?

Reflexive Pronouns

The reflexive pronoun **siebie**, which has no nominative case form, means *oneself* (including *myself, yourself, himself, herself*), as well as *each other, one another,* as in the following sentences:

Rozmawiają ze sobą.	They are talking with one another.
Nie zapominaj o sobie.	Don't forget about yourself.

Nom.	—
Gen.	**siebie, się**
Dat.	**sobie, se**
Acc.	**siebie, się**
Instr.	**sobą**
Loc.	**sobie**

As noted, the use of dative **se** is highly colloquial.

Distributive Pronouns

The plural of the distributive pronoun **każdy każda każde** *each, every* is supplied by **wszyscy wszystkie** *all.*

	Masc.	Fem.	Neut.	Masc.Pers.Pl.	Other Pl.
Nom.	**każdy**	**każda**	**każde**	**wszyscy**	**wszystkie**
Gen.	**każdego**	**każdej**	**każdego**	**wszystkich**	**wszystkich**
Dat.	**każdemu**	**każdej**	**każdemu**	**wszystkim**	**wszystkim**
Acc.	= Nom./Gen.	**każdą**	= Nom.	= Gen.	= Nom.
Instr.	**każdym**	**każdą**	**każdym**	**wszystkimi**	**wszystkimi**
Loc.	**każdym**	**każdej**	**każdym**	**wszystkich**	**wszystkich**

The negative of **każdy każda każde** is **żaden żadna żadne** *no, none, not any*; it is always accompanied by **nie**.

Każdy stół jest zajęty.	Every table is occupied.
Żaden stół nie jest zajęty.	No table is occupied.

4. Adjectives

Declension of Adjectives

Adjectives have different forms that correspond to noun genders, as well as a complete set of case endings in both the singular and plural (except for the vocative plural, which is the same as the nominative). An adjective agrees with the noun it modifies in gender, case, and number. The masculine nominative singular ending is -y: **dobry** *good,* **ladny** *pretty,* **miły** *nice, kind.* After **k** and **g**, the ending is -i: **wielki** *great,* **drogi** *dear, expensive.* It is also -i after soft consonants (which are not common): **tani** (stem **tań-**) *cheap,* **głupi** (stem **głup'-**) *stupid.* The feminine singular ending is -a: **dobra, ladna, miła.** The neuter singular ending is -e: **dobre, ladne, miłe;** after **k** and **g**, it is -ie: **wielkie, drogie.** This is also the plural ending for adjectives modifying non-masculine personal nouns. The masculine personal plural adjective ending is -y/-i and the preceding consonant is softened: **dobry** → **dobrzy, ladny** → **ladni, miły** → **mili, wielki** → **wielcy, drogi** → **drodzy;** for more examples, see below.

	Singular	Plural
Masc.	dobry hotel	dobre hotele
	good hotel	*good hotels*
Masc.pers.	dobry chłopiec	dobrzy mężczyźni
	good boy	*good men*
Fem.	dobra dziewczyna	dobre kobiety
	good girl	*good women*
Neut.	dobre dziecko	dobre krzesła
	good child	*good chairs*

Here is the complete declension of plain-stem adjective **dobry** *good:*

	Masc.	Fem.	Neut.	Masc.Pers.Pl.	Other Pl.
Nom./Voc.	dobry	dobra	dobre	dobrzy	dobre
Gen.	dobrego	dobrej	dobrego	dobrych	dobrych
Dat.	dobremu	dobrej	dobremu	dobrym	dobrym
Acc.	= Nom./Gen.	dobrą	dobre	dobrych	dobre
Instr.	dobrym	dobrą	dobrym	dobrymi	dobrymi
Loc.	dobrym	dobrej	dobrym	dobrych	dobrych

Here is the complete declension of velar-stem adjective **drogi** *dear, expensive*:

	Masc.	Fem.	Neut.	Masc.Pers.Pl.	Other Pl.
Nom./Voc.	drogi	droga	drogie	drodzy	drogie
Gen.	drogiego	drogiej	drogiego	drogich	drogich
Dat.	drogiemu	drogiej	drogiemu	drogim	drogim
Acc.	= Nom./Gen.	drogą	drogie	drogich	drogie
Instr.	drogim	drogą	drogim	drogimi	drogimi
Loc.	drogim	drogiej	drogim	drogich	drogich

Here is the complete declension of soft-stem adjective **tani** *cheap*:

	Masc.	Fem.	Neut.	Masc.Pers.Pl.	Other Pl.
Nom./Voc.	tani	tania	tanie	tani	tanie
Gen.	taniego	taniej	taniego	tanich	tanich
Dat.	taniemu	taniej	taniemu	tanim	tanim
Acc.	=Nom./Gen.	tanią	tanie	tanich	tanie
Instr.	tanim	tanią	tanim	tanimi	tanimi
Loc.	tanim	taniej	tanim	tanich	tanich

Here is a list of adjectives with various stem consonants. Each is followed by its masculine personal plural form, illustrating the various stem-consonant replacements.

b	słaby *weak*	słabi	p	tępy *dull*	tępi
c	lśniący *glistening*	lśniący	p'	głupi *stupid*	głupi
ch	lichy *miserable*	lisi	r	chory *sick*	chorzy
d	młody *young*	młodzi	s	łasy *greedy*	łasi
dz	cudzy *foreign*	cudzy	sł	kisły *sour*	kiśli
g	drogi *dear*	drodzy	sn	własny *own*	właśni
k	wysoki *tall*	wysocy	st	gęsty *thick*	gęści
ł	miły *nice*	mili	sz	starszy *older*	starsi
m	stromy *steep*	stromi	t	bogaty *rich*	bogaci
n	ładny *pretty*	ładni	w	łatwy *easy*	łatwi
ń	tani *cheap*	tani	zł	zły *bad*	źli

Adjective-Noun Order

As in English, a Polish adjective is usually placed before the noun it modifies: **pracowity urzędnik** *hard-working clerk,* **ciężka walizka** *heavy suitcase,* **wysokie drzewo** *tall tree.* However, if an adjective describes the noun as a particular type or class of thing rather than as having some characteristic, the adjective often follows the noun: **Bank Handlowy** *Trade Bank,*

roślina wodna *aquatic plant.* An adjective may also follow the noun in set expressions: **dzień dobry** *hello,* **język polski** *the Polish language.*

Comparison of Adjectives

The comparative form of most common adjectives is obtained by adding the suffix **-szy** (masc.), **-sza** (fem.), and **-sze** (neut.) to the adjective stem, possibly softening the stem consonant. The superlative form is created by adding the prefix **naj-** to the comparative form. Comparative and superlative adjectives have a complete set of endings, like any adjective:

miły *nice, kind*

Nom.sg.	Masc.	**milszy** *kinder*	**najmilszy** *kindest*
	Fem.	**milsza**	**najmilsza**
	Neut.	**milsze**	**najmilsze**
	Masc.pers.pl.	**milsi**	**najmilsi**
	Other Pl.	**milsze**	**najmilsze**

... and so on, for the other case/number endings.

Adjectives ending in consonants plus **-ny** often use the suffix **-iejszy** to form the comparative: **ładny** *pretty,* **ładniejszy** *prettier,* **najładniejszy** *prettiest*; **smutny** *sad,* **smutniejszy** *sadder,* **najsmutniejszy** *saddest.*

The following adjectives have irregular comparative and superlative forms:

dobry *good*	**lepszy** *better*	**najlepszy** *best*
duży *big*	**większy** *bigger*	**największy** *biggest*
mały *small*	**mniejszy** *smaller*	**najmniejszy** *smallest*
zły *bad*	**gorszy** *worse*	**najgorszy** *worst*

Some adjectives and all participles (verbal adjectives) form the comparative and superlative periphrastically, using **bardziej** *more* and **najbardziej** *most.*

chory *sick*	**bardziej chory** *sicker*	**najbardziej chory** *sickest*
zajęty *busy*	**bardziej zajęty** *busier*	**najbardziej zajęty** *busiest*
zmęczony *tired*	**bardziej zmęczony** *more tired*	**najbardziej zmęczony** *most tired*

Adjectives of lesser comparison are formed with **mniej** *less* and **najmniej** *least*: **interesujący** *interesting,* **mniej interesujący** *less interesting,* **najmniej interesujący** *least interesting.*

Adjective Opposites and Their Comparatives

Here is a list of common adjectives, arranged in pairs of opposites. The comparative forms (*more beautiful, uglier,* etc.) are given on the right.

	Positive	Comparative
beautiful, ugly	**piękny, brzydki**	**piękniejszy, brzydszy**
big/large, little/small	**duży, mały**	**większy, mniejszy**
clean, dirty	**czysty, brudny**	**czystszy, brudniejszy**
deep, shallow	**głęboki, płytki**	**głębszy, płytszy**
dense, sparse	**gęsty, rzadki**	**gęstszy, rzadszy**
diligent, lazy	**pracowity, leniwy**	**bardziej pracowity, bardziej leniwy**
dry, wet	**suchy, mokry**	**bardziej suchy, bardziej mokry**
early, late	**wczesny, późny**	**wcześniejszy, późniejszy**
easy, hard	**łatwy, trudny**	**łatwiejszy, trudniejszy**
expensive, cheap	**drogi, tani**	**droższy, tańszy**
far, near	**daleki, bliski**	**dalszy, bliższy**
fast, slow	**szybki, wolny**	**szybszy, wolniejszy**
fat, thin	**gruby, cienki**	**grubszy, cieńszy**
first, last	**pierwszy, ostatni**	—
flat, steep	**płaski, stromy**	**bardziej płaski, bardziej stromy**
free, busy	**wolny, zajęty**	**—, bardziej zajęty**
frequent, rare	**częsty, rzadki**	**częstszy, rzadszy**
full, empty	**pełny, pusty**	**pełniejszy, bardziej pusty**
funny, sad	**śmieszny, smutny**	**śmieszniejszy, smutniejszy**
good, bad	**dobry, zły**	**lepszy, gorszy**
great, small	**wielki, mały**	**większy, mniejszy**
happy, sad	**szczęśliwy, smutny**	**weselszy, smutniejszy**
hard, soft	**twardy, miękki**	**twardszy, miększy**
heavy, light	**ciężki, lekki**	**cięższy, lżejszy**
high, low	**wysoki, niski**	**wyższy, niższy**
hot, cold	**gorący, zimny**	**gorętszy, zimniejszy**
interesting, boring	**ciekawy, nudny**	**ciekawszy, nudniejszy**
light, dark	**jasny, ciemny**	**jaśniejszy, ciemniejszy**
long, short	**długi, krótki**	**dłuższy, krótszy**
new, old	**nowy, stary**	**nowszy, starszy**
open, shut	**otwarty, zamknięty**	—
past, future	**przeszły, przyszły**	—
public, private	**publiczny, prywatny**	—
rich, poor	**bogaty, biedny**	**bogatszy, biedniejszy**
right, wrong	**słuszny, błędny**	**słuszniejszy, bardziej błędny**
right(-hand), left	**prawy, lewy**	—

	Positive	Comparative
sharp, dull	ostry, tępy	ostrzejszy, bardziej tępy
sick, well	chory, zdrowy	bardziej chory, zdrowszy
simple, complex	prosty, złożony	prostszy, bardziej złożony
smart, stupid	mądry, głupi	mądrzejszy, głupszy
smooth, rough	gładki, szorstki	gładszy, bardziej szorstki
straight, crooked	prosty, kręty	prostszy, bardziej kręty
strong, weak	silny, słaby	silniejszy, słabszy
sweet, bitter	słodki, gorzki	słodszy, bardziej gorzki
sweet, sour	słodki, kwaśny	słodszy, kwaśniejszy
tall, short	wysoki, niski	wyższy, niższy
thick, thin	gęsty, rzadki	gęstszy (gęściejszy), rzadszy
urban, rural	miejski, wiejski	—
warm, cool	ciepły, chłodny	cieplejszy, chłodniejszy
wide, narrow	szeroki, wąski	szerszy, węższy
young, old	młody, stary	młodszy, starszy

Many adjective opposites are formed with the prefix **nie-** *un-*.

discriminating, non-discriminating	wybredny, niewybredny
distinct, indistinct	wyraźny, niewyraźny
exact, inexact	ścisły, nieścisły
fresh, stale	świeży, nieświeży
gracious, ungracious	łaskawy, niełaskawy
honest, dishonest	uczciwy, nieuczciwy
intentional, unintentional	umyślny, nieumyślny
interesting, uninteresting	ciekawy, nieciekawy
lucky, unlucky	szczęśliwy, nieszczęśliwy
polite, impolite	grzeczny, niegrzeczny

Almost any adjective can be negated with **nie-**; for example, **niedobry** means *not exactly bad, but not good either.*

5. Adverbs

Formation of Adverbs

Adverbs formed from adjectives end in -o or -'e (with e preceded by softening of the stem consonant): **gęsto** *thickly,* from **gęsty** *thick;* **tanio** *cheaply,* from **tani** *cheap;* **drogo** *dearly,* from **drogi** *dear;* **dobrze** *well,* from **dobry** *good;* **źle** *badly,* from **zły** *bad.* Generally speaking, adverbs formed from adjectives whose stems end in a soft consonant or in **k, g,** or **ch,** end in -o; most others, especially adverbs formed from adjectives whose stems end in a consonant plus -ny, end in -'e. However, many—or even most—common adjectives form adverbs in -o, regardless of the general pattern (see **gęsto** above). Adverbs have comparative and superlative forms in -'ej and naj- + -'ej, respectively: **ciepły** *warm,* **ciepło** *warmly,* **cieplej** *more warmly,* **najcieplej** *most warmly.*

Some adverb formations are irregular. Here are the positive and comparative adverbial forms of some common adjectives:

Adjective	Adverb	Comparative	Superlative
biedny *poor*	biednie	biedniej	najbiedniej
bliski *near*	blisko	bliżej	najbliżej
błędny *wrong*	błędnie	błędniej	najbłędniej
bogaty *rich*	bogato	bogaciej	najbogaciej
brudny *dirty*	brudno	brudniej	najbrudniej
brzydki *ugly*	brzydko	brzydziej	najbrzydziej
chłodny *cool*	chłodno	chłodniej	najchłodniej
chory *sick*	choro	bardziej choro	najbardziej choro
ciekawy *interesting*	ciekawie	ciekawiej	najciekawiej
ciemny *dark*	ciemno	ciemniej	najciemniej
cienki *thin*	cienko	cieniej	najcieniej
ciepły *warm*	ciepło	cieplej	najcieplej
ciężki *heavy, difficult*	ciężko	ciężej	najciężej
częsty *frequent*	często	częściej	najczęściej
czysty *clean*	czysto	czyściej	najczyściej
daleki *far, distant*	daleko	dalej	najdalej
długi *long*	długo	dłużej	najdłużej
dobry *good*	dobrze	lepiej	najlepiej
drogi *dear, expensive*	drogo	drożej	najdrożej

Adjective	Adverb	Comparative	Superlative
duży *large, big*	dużo	więcej	najwięcej
gęsty *thick*	gęsto	gęściej	najgęściej
gładki *smooth*	gładko	gładziej	najgładziej
głęboki *deep*	głęboko	głębiej	najgłębiej
głupi *stupid*	głupio	głupiej	najgłupiej
gorący *hot*	gorąco	goręcej	najgoręcej
gorzki *bitter*	gorzko	bardziej gorzko	najbardziej gorzko
gruby *thick, fat*	grubo	grubiej	najgrubiej
jasny *clear*	jasno/jaśnie	jaśniej	najjaśniej
krótki *short*	krótko	krócej	najkrócej
kwaśny *sour*	kwaśnie	kwaśniej	najkwaśniej
lekki *light*	lekko	lżej	najlżej
leniwy *lazy*	leniwie	leniwiej	najleniwiej
łatwy *easy*	łatwo	łatwiej	najłatwiej
mały *small, little*	mało	mniej	najmniej
mądry *wise*	mądrze	mądrzej	najmądrzej
miękki *soft*	miękko	bardziej miękko	najbardziej miękko
młody *young*	młodo	młodziej	najmłodziej
mokry *wet*	mokro	bardziej mokro	najbardziej mokro
niski *low, short*	nisko	niżej	najniżej
nowy *new*	nowo	bardziej nowo	najbardziej nowo
nudny *boring*	nudno	nudniej	najnudniej
ostry *sharp*	ostro	ostrzej	najostrzej
otwarty *open*	otwarcie	bardziej otwarcie	najbardziej otwarcie
pełny *full*	pełno	pełniej	najpełniej
piękny *beautiful*	pięknie	piękniej	najpiękniej
płaski *flat*	płasko	bardziej płasko	najbardziej płasko
płytki *shallow*	płytko	płycej	najpłycej
późny *late*	późno	później	najpóźniej
pracowity *industrious*	pracowicie	bardziej pracowicie	najbardziej pracowicie
prosty *simple*	prosto	prościej	najprościej
pusty *empty*	pusto	puściej, bardziej pusto	najpuściej, najbardziej pusto
rzadki *rare*	rzadko	rzadziej	najrzadziej
silny *strong*	silno, silnie	silniej	najsilniej
słaby *weak*	słabo	słabiej	najsłabiej
słodki *sweet*	słodko	bardziej słodko	najbardziej słodko

Adjective	Adverb	Comparative	Superlative
słuszny *right, correct*	słusznie	słuszniej	najsłuszniej
smutny *sad*	smutno	smutniej	najsmutniej
stary *old*	staro	starzej	najstarzej
stromy *steep*	stromo	stromiej, bardziej stromo	najstromiej, najbardziej stromo
suchy *dry*	sucho	bardziej sucho	najbardziej sucho
szeroki *wide*	szeroko	szerzej	najszerzej
szorstki *rough*	szorstko	bardziej szorstko	najbardziej szorstko
szybki *quick, fast*	szybko	szybciej	najszybciej
śmieszny *funny*	śmiesznie	śmieszniej	najśmieszniej
tani *cheap*	tanio	taniej	najtaniej
tępy *dull*	tępo	tępiej	najtępiej
trudny *difficult*	trudno	trudniej	najtrudniej
twardy *hard*	twardo	twardziej	najtwardziej
wąski *narrow*	wąsko	wężej	najwężej
wczesny *early*	wcześnie	wcześniej	najwcześniej
wesoły *merry, gay*	wesoło	weselej	najweselej
wielki *great*	wielce	więcej	najwięcej
wolny *slow*	wolno	wolniej	najwolniej
wysoki *tall, high*	wysoko	wyżej	najwyżej
zdrowy *healthy*	zdrowo	zdrowiej	najzdrowiej
zimny *cold*	zimno	zimniej	najzimniej
zły *bad*	źle	gorzej	najgorzej

It is helpful to think of adjectival adverbs as being the gender-neutral form of the adjective, used when there is no specific noun with which the adjective agrees. This includes references to weather or general surroundings.

Jest tu bardzo duszno.	It's very muggy here.
Zawsze jest przyjemnie z tobą rozmawiać.	It's always pleasant to chat with you.
Łatwiej jest jechać samochodem.	It's easier to go by car.

The verbs **czuć się** *feel* and **wyglądać** *look, appear* take the adverbial form.

Bardzo źle się czuję.	I feel very bad.
Ona wygląda bardzo młodo.	She looks very young.

Words that often occur with comparatives, both adjectival and adverbial, are **jeszcze** *even more,* **coraz** *more and more,* and **o wiele** *by a lot.*

Ten dom jest duży, ale tamten jest jeszcze większy.	That house is big, but that other one is even bigger.
Ona wygląda coraz młodziej.	She looks younger and younger.
Klimat robi się coraz cieplejszy.	The weather is getting warmer and warmer.
Ten nóż jest o wiele ostrzejszy, niż tamten.	That knife is a lot sharper than that other one.

Non-Adjectival Adverbs

Non-adjectival adverbs play an important role in Polish speech. Here is a list of important non-adjectival adverbs and adverbial phrases:

already, yet	**już**
always	**zawsze**
before, earlier	**przedtem**
everywhere	**wszędzie**
for how long?	**na jak długo?**
for how much?	**za ile?**
for some reason	**z jakiegoś powodu**
for what reason?	**po co?**
from there/then	**odtąd**
from where?	**skąd?**
hardly ever	**rzadko kiedy**
here	**tu, tutaj**
how	**jak**
how come?	**czemu?**
how much/many?	**ile?**
how often?	**jak często?**
in a moment	**chwileczkę**
never	**nigdy**
now	**teraz**
nowhere	**nigdzie**
often	**często**
once	**raz, kiedyś**
rarely	**rzadko**
rather	**dość**
right away	**zaraz**
since when?	**od kiedy?**
so much, so many	**tyle**
somehow	**jakoś**
sometime, once	**kiedyś**
sometimes	**czasami**
soon	**niedługo**
sooner or later	**prędzej czy później**

still, yet	**jeszcze**
that way	**tamtędy**
then	**wtedy**
then, later	**potem**
there	**tam**
this way	**tędy**
to here, to there	**dotąd**
today	**dziś, dzisiaj**
tomorrow	**jutro**
too, too much	**zbyt**
usually	**zwykle**
what for?	**po co?**
when?	**kiedy?**
whenever	**kiedykolwiek**
where?	**gdzie?**
where to?	**dokąd?**
which way?	**którędy?**
why?	**dlaczego?**
yesterday	**wczoraj**

Notes

The negative forms **nigdzie** *nowhere* and **nigdy** *never* require a negated verb.

On nigdy mnie nie rozumie.	He never understands me.

The adverbs **jeszcze** *still, yet* and **już** *already, yet* are functional opposites, according to whether or not they are negated.

—**Czy jeszcze pracujesz?**	"Are you still working?"
—**Nie, już nie pracuję.**	"No, I'm not working anymore."
—**Czy już jesteś gotowy?**	"Are you ready yet?"
—**Nie, jeszcze nie jestem gotowy.**	"No, I'm not ready yet."

Similarly, **dość** *rather* and **nie zbyt** *not too* are often functional opposites.

Ona jest dość miła.	She is rather nice.
Ona nie jest zbyt miła.	She is not especially nice.

6. Numerals

Cardinal Numerals

In the list below, the forms in parentheses are both the genitive/accusative
and masculine personal forms of the numeral, except as noted.

0   zero
1   jeden, jedna, jedno
2   dwa (dwaj; fem. dwie)
3   trzy (trzej)
4   cztery (czterej)
5   pięć (pięciu)
6   sześć (sześciu)
7   siedem (siedmiu)
8   osiem (ośmiu)
9   dziewięć (dziewięciu)
10 dziesięć (dziesięciu)
11 jedenaście (jedenastu)
12 dwanaście (dwunastu)
13 trzynaście (trzynastu)
14 czternaście (czternastu)
15 piętnaście (piętnastu)
16 szesnaście (szesnastu)
17 siedemnaście (siedemnastu)
18 osiemnaście (osiemnastu)
19 dziewiętnaście (dziewiętnastu)
20 dwadzieścia (dwudziestu)
21 dwadzieścia jeden (dwudziestu jeden)
22 dwadzieścia dwa (dwudziestu dwóch)
23 dwadzieścia trzy (dwudziestu trzech)
24 dwadzieścia cztery (dwudziestu czterech)
25 dwadzieścia pięć (dwudziestu pięciu)
26 dwadzieścia sześć (dwudziestu sześciu)
27 dwadzieścia siedem (dwudziestu siedmiu)
28 dwadzieścia osiem (dwudziestu ośmiu)
29 dwadzieścia dziewięć (dwudziestu dziewięciu)
30 trzydzieści (trzydziestu)
40 czterdzieści (czterdziestu)

50	pięćdziesiąt (pięćdziesięciu)
60	sześćdziesiąt (sześćdziesięciu)
70	siedemdziesiąt (siedemdziesięciu)
80	osiemdziesiąt (osiemdziesięciu)
90	dziewięćdziesiąt (dziewięćdziesięciu)
100	sto (stu)
200	dwieście (dwustu)
300	trzysta (trzystu)
400	czterysta (czterystu)
500	pięćset (pięciuset)
600	sześćset (sześciuset)
700	siedemset (siedmiuset)
800	osiemset (ośmiuset)
900	dziewięćset (dziewięciuset)
1,000	tysiąc
2,000	dwa tysiące
10,000	dziesięć tysięcy
1,000,000	milion
1,000,000,000	miliard

In counting, the word **raz** *once* is used instead of **jeden: raz, dwa, trzy,** and so on.

Cardinal Numeral Syntax

The Polish numeral system strikes most people as complex. Indeed, it has probably never been exhaustively described, and usage can vary from speaker to speaker. Still, the basic outline of the system is easily stated.

1. **The numeral 1.** The numeral 1 has the same endings as **ten ta to** *this/ that*: **jeden koń** *one horse,* **jedna krowa** *one cow,* **jedno drzewo** *one tree.*

2. **The numerals 2, 3, and 4.** In the nominative case, the numerals 2 (masc./ neut. **dwa,** fem. **dwie,** masc.pers. **dwaj**), 3 (**trzy,** masc.pers. **trzej**), and 4 (**cztery,** masc.pers. **czterej**) use the plural form of the counted noun: **dwa konie** *two horses,* **dwie krowy** *two cows,* **dwaj chłopcy** *two boys.* The numerals 2, 3, and 4 take plural verb agreement.

Dwa konie stały.	Two horses were standing.
Czterej chłopcy się bawili.	Four boys were playing.

The masculine personal forms **dwaj, trzej,** and **czterej** occur more often in writing. In speech, they are often replaced by the genitive forms **dwóch, trzech,** and **czterech** plus the genitive plural of the counted noun.

3. **The numerals 5 and above.** The numerals 5 and above are followed by the genitive plural of the counted noun, as though one were saying, for ex-

ample, *five of horses*: **pięć koni** *five horses,* **sześć krów** *six cows,* **siedem piór** *seven pens.* The masculine personal forms of numerals 5 and above end in **-u**, like the genitive/accusative.

	Masc./Fem./Neut.	Masc.Pers.	Masc.Pers. Examples
5	**pięć**	**pięciu**	**pięciu mężczyzn** *5 men*
10	**dziesięć**	**dziesięciu**	**dziesięciu chłopców** *10 boys*

The numerals 5 and above take neuter singular verb agreement.

Pięć książek leżało.	Five books were lying.
Sześciu studentów uczyło się.	Six students were studying.

Predicate adjectives are in the genitive plural.

Siedmiu studentów jest gotowych.	Seven students are ready.

Before non-masculine personal subjects, possessive pronouns are in the nominative or genitive plural. Compare the following sentences:

Moje pięć sióstr jest zamężnych.	My five sisters are married.
Moich pięciu braci jest żonatych.	My five brothers are married.

Such constructions are felt to be awkward and are often avoided.

4. **Compound numerals.** With compound numerals, the counted noun has the case indicated by the final numeral. Numerals ending in 2, 3, or 4 are followed by the nominative plural, while numerals ending in 5, 6, 7, 8, 9, or 0 are followed by the genitive plural: **dwadzieścia trzy zeszyty** *23 notebooks,* **dwadzieścia pięć zeszytów** *25 notebooks.* Compound numerals ending in 1 always end in **jeden**, no matter what the gender of the noun is, and are followed by the genitive plural and take neuter singular verb agreement.

Dwadzieścia jeden zeszytów zostało.	Twenty-one notebooks remained.

Dwaj, trzej, and **czterej** are not used in compound numerals: **dwudziestu dwóch chłopców** *22 boys* (not *dwadzieścia dwaj chłopcy).

Cardinal Numeral Declension

1. **The numeral 1.** The numeral 1, **jeden, jedna, jedno**, is declined like a pronominal adjective (like **ten, ta, to**). It agrees with the noun it modifies in gender, case, and number: **jeden kot** *one cat,* gen.sg. **jednego kota**; **jedna**

krowa *one cow,* gen.sg. **jednej krowy**; **jedno dziecko** *one child,* gen.sg. **jednego dziecka**. The plural form **jedne** is used with plural-only nouns: **jedne drzwi** *one door*. **Jeden, jedna, jedno** is also used in the sense of *a certain*: **jeden człowiek** *a certain man*. In this sense, it may be used in the plural: **jedni ludzie** *some people*.

2. The numerals 2, 3, 4 and *both*.

dwa, dwie, dwa *two*

	Masc./Neut.	Fem.	Masc.Pers.
Nom./Voc.	dwa	dwie	dwaj
Gen./Loc.	dwóch/dwu	dwóch/dwu	dwóch/dwu
Dat.	dwom/dwóm/dwu	dwom/dwóm/dwu	dwom/dwóm/dwu
Acc.	dwa	dwie	dwóch/dwu
Instr.	dwoma	dwiema	dwoma

Dative **dwóm** is considered substandard, but is often heard. **Dwu** is also possible in the instrumental case, but **dwoma, dwiema, dwoma** are the usual forms.

trzy, trzej *three*

	Masc./Fem./Neut.	Masc.Pers.
Nom./Voc.	trzy	trzej
Gen./Loc.	trzech	trzech
Dat.	trzem	trzem
Acc.	trzy	trzech
Instr.	trzema	trzema

cztery, czterej *four*

	Masc./Fem./Neut.	Masc.Pers.
Nom./Voc.	cztery	czterej
Gen./Loc.	czterech	czterech
Dat.	czterem	czterem
Acc.	cztery	czterech
Instr.	czterema	czterema

oba, obie, obaj *both*

	Masc./Neut.	Fem.	Masc.Pers.
Nom./Voc.	oba	obie	obaj
Gen./Loc.	obu	obu	obu
Dat.	obu	obu	obu
Acc.	oba	obie	obu
Instr.	oboma	obiema	oboma

Obu is also possible in the instrumental case, although **oboma, obiema, oboma** are more frequent.

Notes on *dwa, trzy, cztery,* and *oba*

a. The forms **dwaj, trzej, czterej,** and **obaj** are masculine personal forms only. When referring to mixed-gender groups, the collective numeral is commonly used; see Collective Numerals below. The genitive forms **dwóch, trzech, czterech,** and **obu** (plus the genitive plural of the counted noun) suggest a possible mixed-gender group, but do not require it; it could also be all-male.

b. The form **dwu** is possible in the genitive, dative, locative, and instrumental cases, and it is optional, alongside **dwóch,** in the accusative of masculine persons.

c. **Dwom** is the recommended written dative form of **dwa** in all genders, but **dwóm** frequently occurs and **dwu** is also acceptable.

d. **Dwiema** and **obiema** are usual in the feminine instrumental case, alongside optional **dwoma, oboma** and **dwu, obu.**

e. In masculine personal nominative case functions, the forms **dwóch** (or **dwu**), **trzech,** and **czterech** plus the genitive of the counted noun may be used as alternatives to **dwaj, trzej,** and **czterej,** respectively; hence, either **dwaj chłopcy** or **dwóch (dwu) chłopców** *two boys* may be used. The nominative forms **dwaj, trzej,** and **czterej** tend to be used more in writing, the genitive forms more in speech. To summarize:

Male only	**dwaj studenci** *two (male) students*
Possibly mixed gender	**dwóch (dwu) studentów** *two (male or female) students*
Mixed gender	**dwoje studentów** *two students (one male, one female)*

For the form **dwoje,** see Collective Numerals below.

f. **Obydwa, obydwie, obydwaj** is more often used than **oba, obie, obaj**.

3. **The numerals 5 to 90.**

pięć, pięciu *five*

	Masc./Fem./Neut.	Masc.Pers.
Nom./Voc.	pięć	pięciu
Gen./Dat./Loc.	pięciu	pięciu
Acc.	pięć	pięciu
Instr.	pięcioma/pięciu	pięcioma/pięciu

The numerals **sześć, sześciu** *six,* **siedem, siedmiu** *seven,* **osiem, ośmiu** *eight,* **dziewięć, dziewięciu** *nine,* and **dziesięć, dziesięciu** *ten* are declined like **pięć, pięciu.**

jedenaście, jedenastu *eleven*

	Masc./Fem./Neut.	Masc.Pers.
Nom./Voc.	jedenaście	jedenastu
Gen./Dat./Loc.	jedenastu	jedenastu
Acc.	jedenaście	jedenastu
Instr.	jedenastoma/jedenastu	jedenastoma/jedenastu

dwanaście, dwunastu *twelve*

	Masc./Fem./Neut.	Masc.Pers.
Nom./Voc.	dwanaście	dwunastu
Gen./Dat./Loc.	dwunastu	dwunastu
Acc.	dwanaście	dwunastu
Instr.	dwunastoma/dwunastu	dwunastoma/dwunastu

Note the change of **dwa-** to **dwu-** in the oblique case forms of **dwanaście** and of **dwadzieścia** *twenty,* described below: **dwunastu, dwudziestu.** The numerals **trzynaście, trzynastu** *thirteen,* **czternaście, czternastu** *fourteen,* **piętnaście, piętnastu** *fifteen,* **szesnaście, szesnastu** *sixteen,* **siedemnaście, siedemnastu** *seventeen,* **osiemnaście, osiemnastu** *eighteen,* and **dziewiętnaście, dziewiętnastu** *nineteen* are declined like **jedenaście, jedenastu.**

dwadzieścia, dwudziestu *twenty*

	Masc./Fem./Neut.	Masc.Pers.
Nom./Voc.	dwadzieścia	dwudziestu
Gen./Dat./Loc.	dwudziestu	dwudziestu
Acc.	dwadzieścia	dwudziestu
Instr.	dwudziestoma/dwudziestu	dwudziestoma/ dwudziestu

trzydzieści, trzydziestu *thirty*

	Masc./Fem./Neut.	Masc.Pers.
Nom./Voc.	trzydzieści	trzydziestu
Gen./Dat./Loc.	trzydziestu	trzydziestu
Acc.	trzydzieści	trzydziestu
Instr.	trzydziestoma/trzydziestu	trzydziestoma/trzydziestu

The numeral **czterdzieści, czterdziestu** *forty* is declined like **trzydzieści, trzydziestu.**

pięćdziesiąt, pięćdziesięciu *fifty*

	Masc./Fem./Neut.	Masc.Pers.
Nom./Voc.	pięćdziesiąt	pięćdziesięciu
Gen./Dat./Loc.	pięćdziesięciu	pięćdziesięciu
Acc.	pięćdziesiąt	pięćdziesięciu
Instr.	pięćdziesięcioma/ pięćdziesięciu	pięćdziesięcioma/ pięćdziesięciu

The numerals **sześćdziesiąt** ("szeździesiąt"), **sześćdziesięciu** *sixty*, **siedemdziesiąt, siedemdziesięciu** *seventy*, **osiemdziesiąt, osiemdziesięciu** *eighty*, and **dziewięćdziesiąt, dziewięćdziesięciu** *ninety* are declined like **pięćdziesiąt, pięćdziesięciu.**

4. The numerals 100 to 900.

sto, stu *hundred*

	Masc./Fem./Neut.	Masc.Pers.
Nom./Acc./Voc.	sto	stu
Gen./Dat./Instr./Loc.	stu	stu
(Optional instr.	stoma	stoma)

dwieście, dwustu *two hundred*

	Masc./Fem./Neut.	Masc.Pers.
Nom./Acc./Voc.	dwieście	dwustu
Gen./Dat./Instr./Loc.	dwustu	dwustu
(Optional instr.	dwustoma	dwustoma)

trzysta, trzystu *three hundred*

	Masc./Fem./Neut.	Masc.Pers.
Nom./Acc./Voc.	trzysta	trzystu
Gen./Dat./Instr./Loc.	trzystu	trzystu
(Optional instr.	trzystoma	trzystoma)

czterysta, czterystu *four hundred*

	Masc./Fem./Neut.	Masc.Pers.
Nom./Acc./Voc.	czterysta	czterystu
Gen./Dat./Instr./Loc.	czterystu	czterystu
(Optional instr.	czterystoma	czterystoma)

The instrumental forms in **-oma** above are optional, alongside forms in **-u**. **Czterysta** has the stress on its first syllable: CZTE-ry-sta.

pięćset, pięciuset *five hundred*

	Masc./Fem./Neut.	Masc.Pers.
Nom./Acc./Voc.	pięćset	pięciuset
Gen./Dat./Instr./Loc.	pięciuset	pięciuset

Note that the instrumental of **pięćset** is **pięciuset** (never *pięciomaset): **z pięciuset pasażerami** *with 500 passengers.* The element **-set** does not trigger stress advancement to the next-to-last syllable: **pięciuset** (PIĘ-ciu-set), **siedemset** (SIE-dem-set), and so on. **Sześćset, sześciuset** *six hundred,* **siedemset, siedmiuset** *seven hundred,* **osiemset, ośmiuset** *eight hundred,* and **dziewięćset, dziewięciuset** *nine hundred* are declined like **pięćset, pięciuset.**

5. Thousand, million.

tysiąc *thousand*

	Singular	Plural
Nom./Voc.	tysiąc	tysiące
Gen.	tysiąca	tysięcy
Dat.	tysiącowi	tysiącom
Acc.	tysiąc	tysiące
Instr.	tysiącem	tysiącami
Loc.	tysiącu	tysiącach

Tysiącu is often heard for the dative singular, but is considered incorrect.

milion *million*

	Singular	Plural
Nom./Voc.	milion	miliony
Gen.	miliona	milionów
Dat.	milionowi	milionom
Acc.	milion	miliony
Instr.	milionem	milionami
Loc.	milionie	milionach

The numerals 1,000, 1,000,000, and so on are declined as regular masculine nouns in both the singular and plural, including when reference is to a masculine personal group: **dwa tysiące zeszytów** *2,000 notebooks*, **pięć milionów ludzi** *5,000,000 people*. In the oblique cases, **tysiąc** and **milion** as head numerals are always followed by the genitive plural of the counted noun.

Ta książka wyszła w kilku tysiącach egzemplarzy.	That book came out in several thousand copies.

Collective Numerals

A set of collective numerals is used with mixed male-female groups, with the young of animals, and with plural-only nouns. In poetic use, collective numerals may be used with paired body parts, such as eyes or hands. Most frequently used are the collective numerals 2 through 12.

2 **dwoje, dwojga**
3 **troje, trojga**
4 **czworo, czworga**
5 **pięcioro, pięciorga**
6 **sześcioro, sześciorga**
7 **siedmioro, siedmiorga**
8 **ośmioro, ośmiorga**

9 dziewięcioro, dziewięciorga
10 dziesięcioro, dziesięciorga
11 jedenaścioro, jedenaściorga
12 dwanaścioro, dwanaściorga

... and so on. Collective forms like **dwadzieścioro** *twenty* and **trzydzieścioro** *thirty* may be used, but are not compounded.

The nominative case of the collective numeral is followed by the genitive plural of the counted noun: **pięcioro dzieci** *five children,* **czworo ludzi** *four people,* **dwoje drzwi** *two doors.* Note that with the numeral 1, plural-only nouns either use the form **jedne** (for example, **jedne drzwi** *one door*) or, if paired, use **para** *pair*: **para nożyczek** *a pair of scissors.*

Here are the declensions of **dwoje** and **pięcioro**, with the case required of the counted noun; the example is with **kurczęta** *chicks.*

Nom./Voc.	dwoje	pięcioro	kurcząt	(gen.pl.)
Gen.	dwojga	pięciorga	kurcząt	(gen.pl.)
Dat.	dwojgu	pięciorgu	kurczętom	(dat.pl.)
Acc.	dwoje	pięcioro	kurcząt	(gen.pl.)
Instr.	dwojgiem	pięciorgiem	kurcząt	(gen.pl.)
Loc.	dwojgu	pięciorgu	kurczętach	(loc.pl.)

Numeral Substantives

Numeral substantives, which are regular feminine nouns ending in **-ka**, are used to refer to items by numerical designation.

1 jedynka
2 dwójka
3 trójka
4 czwórka
5 piątka
6 szóstka
7 siódemka
8 ósemka
9 dziewiątka
10 dziesiątka
11 jedenastka
12 dwunastka

... and so on. For example, **dziesiątka** can refer to room No. 10, a 10-millimeter wrench, or bus No. 10, and **Polska jedenastka** *the Polish eleven* refers to a soccer team. Numeral substantives may be used colloquially in place of collective numerals: **dwójka dzieci** *a couple of kids.*

Indefinite Numerals

The following indefinite and question-word numerals decline like **pięć**:

ile, ilu, iloma	how much, how many; as much, as many
wiele, wielu, wieloma	much, many
kilka, kilku, kilkoma	several
parę, paru, paroma	a couple, several
tyle, tylu, tyloma	so much, so many; as much, as many
kilkanaście, kilkunastu, kilkunastoma	a dozen or so
kilkadziesiąt, kilkudziesięciu, kilkudziesięcioma	several dozen
paręnaście, parunastu, parunastoma	a couple dozen
parędziesiąt, parudziesięciu, parudziesięcioma	several dozen

Counting People

It is most practical to learn to count groups of people in the nominative case. The group may be all male, all non-male, definitely mixed male and female, and possibly mixed male and female. The full range of options occurs only for the numerals 2, 3, and 4 and *both*. Here are the numerals 2 and 5 in the nominative case, using **student(ka)** *student*.

	All Male	All Female	Mixed	Possibly Mixed
2	**dwaj studenci**	**dwie studentki**	**dwoje studentów**	**dwóch studentów**
5	**pięciu studentów**	**pięć studentek**	**pięcioro studentów**	**pięciu studentów**

Ordinal Numerals

The most important uses of ordinal numerals are to tell time, to refer to floors in buildings, and to count items in a series. They have regular adjective endings: **pierwszy pociąg** *first train,* **pierwsza noc** *first night,* **pierwsze piętro** *first floor.*

Ordinal Numerals 1 to 30

The most important ordinal numerals are *first* through *thirty-first.* (This covers all days of the month.)

1st	pierwszy	17th	siedemnasty
2nd	drugi	18th	osiemnasty
3rd	trzeci	19th	dziewiętnasty
4th	czwarty	20th	dwudziesty
5th	piąty	21st	dwudziesty pierwszy
6th	szósty	22nd	dwudziesty drugi
7th	siódmy	23rd	dwudziesty trzeci
8th	ósmy	24th	dwudziesty czwarty
9th	dziewiąty	25th	dwudziesty piąty
10th	dziesiąty	26th	dwudziesty szósty
11th	jedenasty	27th	dwudziesty siódmy
12th	dwunasty	28th	dwudziesty ósmy
13th	trzynasty	29th	dwudziesty dziewiąty
14th	czternasty	30th	trzydziesty
15th	piętnasty	31st	trzydziesty pierwszy
16th	szesnasty		

Note that both elements of a compound ordinal numeral are in the ordinal form, as though one were saying *twentieth-first.*

Other ordinal forms include **czterdziesty** *40th,* **pięćdziesiąty** *50th,* **sześćdziesiąty** *60th,* **siedemdziesiąty** *70th,* **osiemdziesiąty** *80th,* **dziewięćdziesiąty** *90th,* **setny** *100th,* and **tysięczny** *1000th.*

Telling Time

Ordinal numerals are used with **godzina** *hour, o'clock* to tell time (for example, **godzina pierwsza** *one o'clock*) and to give dates (for example, **pierwszy maja** *the first of May*); see below.

"At a given time of day" is expressed by the preposition **o** plus the locative case of **godzina** (which may be omitted), followed by the ordinal numeral: **o (godzinie) pierwszej** *at one o'clock.* Minutes after the hour is expressed by the number of minutes plus the preposition **po** plus the locative case of the hour: **pięć po piątej** *five past five.* Minutes before the hour is expressed by the preposition **za** plus the accusative case of the minutes plus the nominative case of the hour: **za dziesięć siódma** *ten till seven.* Half hours are expressed by **wpół do** *half till* plus the genitive case of the hour: **wpół do dziewiątej** *half till nine, 8:30.* Quarter hours are expressed with **kwadrans: kwadrans po trzeciej** *3:15,* **za kwadrans czwarta** *3:45.* The notions A.M. and P.M. are rendered by the phrases **rano** *in the morning,* **po południu** *in the afternoon,* **wieczorem** *in the evening,* and **nocą** *at night.*

Jest godzina druga rano.	It's 2 A.M.
Film się zaczyna o siódmej **wieczorem.**	The film begins at 7 P.M.

Dates

A stand-alone date is expressed by the masculine form of the ordinal numeral, followed by the genitive of the month: **pierwszy maja** *May 1st,* **jedenasty grudnia** *December 11th.* "On a date" is expressed by putting the entire expression in the genitive; if the numeral is a compound (20 or above), both numerals appear in the ordinal form: **trzydziestego sierpnia** *on August 30th,* **dwudziestego drugiego listopada** *on November 22nd.*

Years

The year is expressed in the following ways:

Stand-alone year	**rok tysiąc dziewięćset sześćdziesiąty drugi** *1962*
"In the year"	**roku tysiąc dziewięćset sześćdziesiątego drugiego** (gen.)
	OR **w roku tysiąc dziewięćset sześćdziesiątym drugim** (loc.)

The genitive construction is used more for historical events.

In giving the year of one's birth, the locative is generally used.

Urodziłem/Urodziłam się	I was born in 1974.
w roku tysiąc dziewięćset	
siedemdziesiątym czwartym.	

The year 2000 is **rok dwutysięczny**; 2001 is **rok dwa tysiące pierwszy**; 2008 is **rok dwa tysiące ósmy.** In oblique cases, **dwa tysiące** is commonly replaced by the ordinal form **dwutysięczny: w roku dwutysięcznym dziewiątym** *in (the year) 2009.*

Expressing "How Old"

In Polish, one asks, "How many years do you have?" (**Ile masz lat?** (formal, **Ile pan(i) ma lat?**)), and answers, "I have so many years."

Mam osiemnaście lat.	I am 18 years old.
Mam sześćdziesiąt jeden lat.	I am 61 years old.

7. Prepositions

In the lists of prepositions below, the case required in the following noun is indicated in parentheses (KEY: gen(itive), dat(ive), acc(usative), instr(umental), loc(ative)).

English-to-Polish Prepositions

about, at (a time)	**o** (+ loc.)
according to	**podług, według** (+ gen.)
across from	**naprzeciw(ko)** (+ gen./dat.)
after	**po** (+ acc./loc.), **za** (+ instr.)
against, opposed to	**przeciw(ko)** (+ dat.)
against, up against	**o** (+ acc.)
(all) around	**dokoła (dookoła), naokoło** (+ gen.)
along, over (the surface of)	**po** (+ loc.)
alongside, next to	**obok** (+ gen.)
among, in the midst of	**pośród, wśród** (+ gen.)
around, about	**koło, około, wokół, wokoło** (+ gen.)
as far as, up to	**po** (+ acc.)
as the result of	**wskutek** (+ gen.)
at	**na** (+ loc.), **przy** (+ loc.), **w(e)** (+ loc.)
at (someone's)	**u** (+ gen.)
because of	**przez(e)** (+ acc.), **z(e)** (+ gen.)
before, in front of	**przed(e)** (+ instr./acc.)
behind, beyond, in back of	**za** (+ acc./instr.)
besides, beyond	**oprócz** (+ gen.), **poza** (+ instr.), **prócz** (+ gen.)
between, among	**między** (+ acc./instr.)
by (the agency of)	**przez(e)** (+ acc.)
despite, in spite of	**mimo** (+ gen.), **wbrew** (+ dat.)
due to, thanks to	**dzięki** (+ dat.)
during	**podczas** (+ gen.), **przy** (+ loc.), **w czasie** (+ gen.)
during the time/reign of	**za** (+ gen.)
for (a time)	**na** (+ acc.)
for (the benefit of)	**dla** (+ gen.)

for, in exchange for	**za** (+ acc.)
for, in favor of	**za** (+ instr.)
from, away from	**od(e)** (+ gen.)
from, out of	**z(e)** (+ gen.)
from among, from out of	**spośród** (+ gen.)
in, at	**w(e)** (+ loc.)
in view of, regarding	**wobec** (+ gen.)
instead of	**zamiast** (+ gen.)
near	**blisko** (+ gen.)
near, next to	**przy** (+ loc.)
off, down from	**z(e)** (+ gen.)
on, at	**na** (+ loc.)
onto, to (a meeting place)	**na** (+ acc.)
out of, from	**z(e)** (+ gen.)
over, above, on top of	**nad(e)** (+acc./instr.)
regarding	**wobec** (+ gen.)
since	**od(e)** (+ gen.)
than	**od(e)** (+ gen.)
through, across; by (the agency of), because of	**przez(e)** (+ acc.)
to, up to, as far as, until	**do** (+ gen.)
toward	**ku** (+ dat.) (*rare*)
under, beneath, below	**pod(e)** (+ acc./instr.)
while	**przy** (+ loc.)
with, having	**o** (+ loc.)
with, together with, along with, accompanied by	**z(e)** (+ instr.)
without	**bez(e)** (+ gen.)

Polish-to-English Prepositions

bez(e) (+ gen.)	without
blisko (+ gen.)	near
dla (+ gen.)	for (the benefit of)
do (+ gen.)	to, up to, as far as, until
dokoła (dookoła) (+ gen.)	(all) around
dzięki (+ dat.)	due to, thanks to
koło, około, wokół, wokoło (+ gen.)	around, about
ku (+ dat.)	toward (*rare*)
między (+ acc.)	(to) between, among
między (+ instr.)	between, among
mimo (+ gen.)	despite, in spite of

na (+ acc.)	onto, to (a meeting place); for (a time)
na (+ loc.)	on, at
nad(e) (+ acc.)	(to) over, above, on top of
nad(e) (+ instr.)	over, above, on top of
naokoło (+ gen.)	all around
naprzeciw(ko) (+ gen.)	across from
o (+ acc.)	against, up against
o (+ loc.)	about, at (a time); with, having
obok (+ gen.)	alongside, next to
od(e) (+ gen.)	from, away from; since; than
oprócz, prócz (+ gen.)	besides, beyond
po (+ acc.)	after; as far as, up to
po (+ loc.)	after; along, over (the surface of)
pod(e) (+ acc.)	(to) under, beneath, below; during
pod(e) (+ instr.)	under, beneath, below
podczas (+ gen.)	during
podług (+ gen.)	according to
pośród (+ gen.)	among
poza (+ instr.)	besides, beyond
przeciw(ko) (+ dat.)	against, opposed to
przed(e) (+ acc.)	(to) before, in front of
przed(e) (+ instr.)	before, in front of
przez(e) (+ acc.)	through, across; by (the agency of), because of
przy (+ loc.)	at, near, next to; while, during
spośród (+ gen.)	from among, out of
u (+ gen.)	at (someone's), near
w(e) (+ acc.)	into (a large area)
w(e) (+ loc.)	in, at
wbrew (+ dat.)	despite
w czasie (+ gen.)	during
według (+ gen.)	according to
wobec (+ gen.)	in view of; regarding
wskutek (+ gen.)	as the result of
wśród (+ gen.)	among, in the midst of
z(e) (+ gen.)	out of, from, off, down from; because of
z(e) (+ instr.)	with, together with, along with, accompanied by
za (+ acc.)	(to) behind, beyond; for, in exchange for
za (+ gen.)	during the time/reign of
za (+ instr.)	behind, beyond, after; for, in favor of
zamiast (+ gen.)	instead of

Prepositions According to the Case Required

Genitive Only

Almost all prepositions that take the genitive case take this case only. Here is a list of most of these prepositions:

bez(e)	without
blisko	near
dla	for (the benefit of)
do	to, up to, as far as, until
dokoła (dookoła)	(all) around
koło, około, wokół, wokoło	around, about
mimo	despite, in spite of
naokoło	all around
naprzeciw(ko)	across from
obok	alongside , next to
od(e)	from, away from; since; than
oprócz, prócz	besides
podczas	during
podług	according to
pośród	among
spośród	from among, out of
u	at (someone's), near
w czasie	during
według	according to
wobec	in view of, regarding
wskutek	as the result of
wśród	among, in the midst of
z(e)	out of, from, down from, off; because of
za	during the time/reign of
zamiast	instead of

Dative Only

Here is a list of the prepositions that take only the dative case:

dzięki	due to, thanks to
ku (*rare*)	toward
przeciw(ko)	against, opposed to
wbrew	despite

Accusative Only

przez(e)   through, across; by (the agency of), because of

Instrumental Only

poza   besides, beyond
z(e)   with, together with, along with, accompanied by

The instrumental preposition **z(e)** should not be confused with its homonym **z(e)** (+ gen.) *out of, from, off.*

Locative Only

przy ·   at, near, next to; while, during

Locative or Accusative

	Locative (State)	**Accusative (Motion)**
na	on, at	onto, to (a meeting place); for (a time)
o	about, at (a time), with*	against, up against
po	after; along, over (the surface of)	after; as far as, up to; for (to get)
w(e)	in, at	into (a large area)

*with in the sense of *characterized by*: **dom o stromym dachu** *house with a steep roof.*

Instrumental or Accusative

	Instrumental (State)	**Accusative (Motion)**
między	between, among	(to) between, among
nad(e)	over, above, on top of	(to) over, above, on top of
pod(e)	under, beneath, below	(to) under, beneath, below; during
przed(e)	before, in front of	(to) before, in front of
za	behind, beyond; for, in favor of	(to) behind, beyond; for, in exchange for

Prepositions that require the instrumental case form genitive-requiring compounds with **z-/s-** to express motion from: **spomiędzy** *from among,* **znad(e)** *from above,* **spod(e)** *from below,* **sprzed(e)** *from in front of,* **zza** *from behind.*

Ta szafa pochodzi sprzed wojny.	That wardrobe dates from before the war.

Prepositions Expressing *at, to,* and *from*

	Location	Motion Toward	Motion From
With people	**u** (+ gen.)	**do** (+ gen.)	**od(e)** (+ gen.)
With containers*	**w(e)** (+ loc.)	**do** (+ gen.)	**z(e)** (+ gen.)
With surfaces, wide-open spaces, and assemblies	**na** (+ loc.)	**na** (+ acc.)	**z(e)** (+ gen.)
Bodies of water	**nad(e)** (+ instr.)	**nad(e)** (+ acc.)	**znad(e)** (+ gen.)
Near towns	**pod(e)** (+ instr.)	**pod(e)** (+ acc.)	**spod(e)** (+ gen.)

containers in the broadest sense, including most things, whether concrete or abstract, and places: **w dobrym nastroju** *in a good mood,* **w Warszawie** *in Warsaw.* Containers with vague boundaries may take **w** (+ acc.) to express motion to: **w las** *into the forest.*

u dentysty / do dentysty / od dentysty	at/to/from the dentist's
w biurze / do biura / z biura	in/to/from the office
na lotnisku / na lotnisko / z lotniska	at/to/from the airport
na koncercie / na koncert / z koncertu	at/to/from the concert
nad morzem / nad morze / znad morza	at/to/from the seaside
pod Warszawą / pod Warszawę / spod Warszawy	near / to near / from near Warsaw

Expressions of Time

Here are expressions using **rok** *year*:

rok (accusative alone) *for a year('s length of time)*
> **Byłem w Polsce jeden rok.**   I was in Poland for a year.

do roku (1) (**do** (+ gen.)) *up to (a specific) year*
> **Do zeszłego roku mieszkałem u rodziców.**   Up until last year, I lived with my parents.

do roku (2) (**do** (+ gen.)) *up to a year('s length of time)*
> **Dostał do roku więzienia.**   He got up to a year in prison.

na rok (1) (**na** (+ acc.)) *for a year (looking ahead)*
> **Wyjeżdżam do Polski na rok.**   I'm going to Poland for a year.

na rok (2) (**na** (+ acc.)) *exactly a year before*
> **Zbieramy się na rok przed obchodami.**   We're gathering a year before the celebration.

o rok (**o** (+ acc.)) *by a year*
> **Przegapiliśmy jubileusz o cały rok.**   We missed the anniversary by an entire year.

od roku (1) (**od** (+ gen.)) *for the year (just past)*
Od roku pracuję jako kelner. For the past year, I've been working
as a waiter.

od roku (2) (**od** (+ gen.)) *since (a specific) year*
Pracuję tam od zeszłego I've been working there since last year.
roku.

po roku (**po** (+ loc.)) *after a year (usually looking back)*
Po tylko jednym roku After only one year, you speak Polish
mówisz zupełnie dobrze quite well.
po polsku.

Compare with **za** (+ acc.).

przed rokiem (1) (**przed** (+ instr.)) *a year ago*
Przeprowadziliśmy się tu We moved here a year ago.
przed rokiem.

przed rokiem (2) (**przed** (+ instr.)) *before (a specific) year*
Przed rokiem Before 1976, I didn't work.
siedemdziesiątym szóstym
nie pracowałem.

This construction is roughly equivalent to **do zeszłego roku** *up to last year.*

przez rok (**przez** (+ acc.)) *through the course of a year*
Byłem chory przez cały rok. I was sick the whole year through.

This construction is usually more emphatic than the accusative alone.

w rok (1) (**w** (+ acc.)) *in the space of a year*
Wszystko zdążyłem zrobić I managed to do everything in the
w rok. space of a year.

More frequently used, with about the same meaning, is **w ciągu roku** *in the course of a year.*

w rok (2) (**w** (+ acc.)) *a year (before)*
To się stało w rok przed That happened a year before Wojtek's
śmiercią Wojtka. death.

w roku (**w** (+ loc.)) *in (a specific) year*
Mam pojechać do Polski w I'm supposed to go to Poland this year.
tym roku.

za rok (**za** (+ acc.)) *after a year (looking ahead)*
Za jeszcze jeden rok będziesz After one more year, you will speak
już mówił po polsku Polish completely fluently.
zupełnie płynnie.

Polish Translations of *for*

The English preposition *for* has a wide variety of translations into Polish, using various prepositions, several cases, and even the conditional tense of the verb. The most important correspondences of English *for* are given below.

1. **dla** (+ gen.)

   for the benefit of
   Czy te kwiaty są dla mnie?   Are those flowers for me?

   (easy/hard) for
   To łatwe dla mnie.   That's easy for me.

   for the sake of
   sztuka dla sztuki   art for art's sake

2. **za** (+ acc.)

   in exchange for
   Ile zapłaciłeś za ten zegarek?   How much did you pay for that watch?
   Sprzedałem za grosze.   I sold it for pennies.

   (responsible) for
   Nie odpowiadam za jego   I'm not responsible for his behavior.
   zachowanie.

   in place of
   Niech ja to zrobię za ciebie.   Let me do that for (instead of) you.

   on behalf of
   za wolność   for freedom

   (mistake/pass) for
   Wziąłem go za lekarza.   I took him for a doctor.
   Uchodził za arystokratę.   He tried to pass for an aristocrat.

   (thank) for
   Dziękuję za pomoc.   Thanks for the help.

   (ask pardon) for
   Przepraszam za kłopot.   Excuse me for the bother.

3. **na** (+ acc.)

   (intended) for
   bilet na samolot   ticket for the airplane
   podręcznik na użytek   textbook for the use of foreigners
   cudzoziemców

(desire) for

| **Mam ochotę na coś zimnego.** | I feel like having something cold. |

for (naught)

To wszystko pójdzie na nic.   That'll all go for nothing.

for (a time or event)

bilet na godzinę ósmą — ticket for eight o'clock
spóźniać się na — to be late for the performance
przedstawienie

for (a time yet to come)

Wyjeżdżam na rok. — I'm leaving for a year.
Rozstajemy się na zawsze. — We're parting forever.

Na (+ acc.) is also used in exclamations like **na miłość boską** *for God's sake!*

4. **od(e)** (+ gen.)

for (a time just past)

Mieszkam w Warszawie od siedmiu lat. — I've been living in Warsaw for the past seven years.

5. **przez(e)** (+ acc.)

for (a period of time)

Przez ostatnie miesiące pracujemy pełną parą. — We've been working at maximum (*lit.*, at full steam) for the last several months.

This sense of *for* may also be expressed by the accusative case without a preposition: **Noszę ten kapelusz już jedenaście lat.** *I've been wearing that hat for 11 years already.* "For periods of time on end" can be expressed by the instrumental without a preposition: **całymi dniami** *for days on end*; **całe dnie** and **przez całe dnie** are also correct.

6. **po** (+ acc.)

(go) for

Wyskoczę po piwo. — I'll dash out for some beer.
Zajadę po ciebie o ósmej. — I'll drop by for you at eight o'clock.

7. **do** (+ gen.)

for (a specific application)

woda do picia — water for drinking
maszynka do ogolenia — electric razor (*lit.*, machine for shaving)
pasta do zębów — toothpaste

8. **o** (+ acc.)

(ask/fight) for
prosić o pomoc	ask for help
walczyć o istnienie/	fight for existence/equality
równouprawnienie	

9. **u** (+ gen.)

for (be employed by)
Ona pracuje u dentysty.	She works for a dentist.

"Work for a company/firm" is expressed by **w** (+ loc.).

Pracuję w banku.	I work for a bank.

10. **jak na** (+ acc.)

for (in a derogatory comparison)
On nieźle mówi jak na	He doesn't speak badly for a foreigner.
cudzoziemca.	

11. **z(e)** (+ gen.)

(known) for
On jest znany ze swoich	He is known for his earlier works.
wcześniejszych prac.	

12. **za** (+ instr.)

(long) for
Tęsknię za tobą.	I miss / long for you.

In archaic Polish, **po** (+ loc.) is used for this expression: **Tęsknię po tobie.**

13. **jeśli chodzi o** (+ acc.), **co do** (+ gen.)

as for
Jeśli chodzi o brata, to on	As for my brother, he is still in school.
jest jeszcze w szkole.	
Co do twojego pomysłu, on	As for your idea, it is totally
jest zupełnie nierealny.	impractical.

14. **The conditional.** The English use of *for* after a verb of request corresponds to Polish use of the conditional.

Prosili, żebyśmy mniej	They asked (for) us to make less noise.
hałasowali.	

8. Conjunctions

Some important Polish coordinating conjunctions are **a** *and, but,* **i** *and,* **i...
i...** *both ... and ...,* **ale** *but,* **albo... albo...** *either ... or ...,* and **ani... ani...**
neither ... nor.... English *and* is usually translated by **i**; however, if there is
any contrast between the items it joins, that is, if *and* can also be *but,* it is
translated by **a**.

Marek jest studentem, a Maria już pracuje.	Marek is a student, but Maria is already working.
Warszawa i Kraków są dość duże.	Warsaw and Krakow are rather large.
Jan jest i inteligentny i przystojny.	Jan is both smart and good-looking.
To jest muzeum, ale nie jest zbyt ciekawe.	That's a museum, but it's not too interesting.
To jest albo szpital, albo hotel.	That's either a hospital or a hotel.
To nie jest ani szpital, ani hotel.	That's neither a hospital nor a hotel.

Important conjunctions introducing subordinate clauses include **chociaż**
although, **bo** *because,* **ponieważ** *since,* **jeśli** *if,* and **to/wtedy** *then.* The most
important subordinating conjunctions are **że** *that* and **czy** *whether.* The conjunction **że** should not be deleted, as it sometimes is in English.

Słyszałem, że masz nową pracę.	I heard (that) you have a new job.

The conjunction **jeśli** *if* is used in the first part of an *if ... then ...* sentence.
It is not used to translate *if* in the sense of *whether*; **czy** is used instead.

Nie wiem, czy (NOT *****jeśli**) **on jest zajęty.**	I don't know whether he is busy.

Questioning adverbs may serve as subordinating conjunctions. Note that
subordinating conjunctions are preceded by a comma.

Czy pamiętasz, gdzie ona mieszka?	Do you remember where she lives?
Nie wiem, jak to powiedzieć.	I don't know how to say that.

Expressing *if ... then ...*

The factual conditional conjunctions are **jeśli** *if* plus either **to** or **wtedy** *then*. *Then* is less often omitted in Polish than it is in English.

Jeśli będziesz tam tak siedzieć przed telewizorem, to ja pójdę spać.	If you're going to sit there in front of the TV, (then) I'm going to bed.

The counterfactual conditional conjunctions are **gdyby** or **jeśliby** *if* plus either **to** or **wtedy** *then*. The element **by** is taken from the conditional form of the verb and may take personal verb endings (**-m, -ś, -śmy, -ście**). See Conditional Mood in Chapter 9. In the counterfactual conditional, the conjunction expressing *then* is often omitted.

Gdybym wiedział, że wybierasz się do miasta, poprosiłbym (OR tobym poprosił) cię zawieźć mnie ze sobą.	If I had known you were headed into town, I would have asked you to take me with you.

Here is a list of important conjunctions and connectives:

although	**chociaż**
and	**i; a**
as soon as	**jak tylko**
as though	**jak gdyby**
as ... as ...	**tak, jak...**
at the time when	**wtedy, kiedy...**
because	**dlatego; że; bo**
before	**zanim**
both ... and ...	**i... i...**
but	**ale; a**
either ... or ...	**albo... albo...**
for, because, since	**bo**
if	**jeśli; gdy**
if ... then ...	**jeśli... to...**
neither ... nor ...	**ani... ani...**
not until	**dopóki nie**
only just	**co dopiero**
or	**albo**
since, as long as	**skoro**
since, for	**ponieważ**
so that, in order to	**żeby; aby**
than	**niż**
that (*subord. conj.*)	**że**
the way that	**tak, jak...**
then	**to; wtedy**

therefore	**dlatego**
until	**zanim**; **aż**
whether	**czy**
whether … or …	**czy… czy…**

9. Verbs

The Infinitive

The infinitive, or dictionary form of the verb, is translated as *"to ask," "to write,"* and so on. Most Polish infinitives end in a vowel plus **-ć**, for example, **pisać** *to write.* Some end in **-ść** or **-źć**, for example, **nieść** *to carry* and **znaleźć** *to find*; a few end in **-c**, for example, **móc** *to be able.* Reflexive verbs are accompanied by the particle **się** *self,* for example, **bać się** *to be afraid.* For the most part, Polish verbs occur in *aspect pairs,* consisting of *imperfective* (impf.) and *perfective* (pf.) partners, for example, **pisać** *write* impf., pf. **napisać**. Details about imperfective and perfective aspect are provided below.

It is common to list a verb in the infinitive and the first- and second-person present tense forms, from which the other forms of the verb can usually be predicted. Often, these present tense forms are abbreviated, for example, **pytać** *-am -asz ask,* which indicates that the verb belongs to the **pytać** *pytam pytasz* verb class, or Class 3. The full verb citation consists of both the imperfective and perfective aspect forms, for example, **pytać** *-am -asz* impf., pf. **zapytać** *ask.*

Finite Verb Categories

Here is a chart of the Polish finite verb system, that is, the categories characterized by tense and/or person. The sample verb is **pisać** *-szę -szesz* impf., pf. **napisać** *write.*

	Imperfective	**Perfective**
Present	**piszę**	—
	I write / am writing	
Past	**pisałem,** fem. **pisałam**	**napisałem,** fem. **napisałam**
	I wrote / was writing	*I wrote, I finished writing*
Future	**będę pisał(a)**	**napiszę**
	I am going to write / be writing	*I'll get written, I'll finish writing*
Imperative	**pisz**	**napisz**
	write, keep writing!	*write! finish writing!*

Pragmatic Personal Verb Categories

Polish uses the titles **pan** *Mr., sir,* **pani** *madam, Mrs., Miss, Ms.,* and **państwo** *ladies and gentlemen, Mr. and Mrs.* plus third-person verb forms as de facto second-person forms of polite address, or "titled address." Titled address is used routinely with strangers, superiors, and casual acquaintances. Practice varies in the workplace, but informal address is the norm among co-workers, as it is among classmates at any educational level. The pragmatic Polish conjugational system is illustrated in the present tense below, but the system applies to the past and future tenses also. The sample verb is **czytać** *-am -asz* impf. *read.*

	Singular	**Plural**
First-person	**(ja) czytam**	**(my) czytamy**
	I read / am reading	*we read / are reading*
Second-person informal	**(ty) czytasz**	**(wy) czytacie**
	you (sg.) read / are reading	*you (pl.) read / are reading*
Second-person formal	**pan (pani) czyta**	**państwo czytają**
	you (sg.) read / are reading	*you (pl.) read / are reading*
Third-person	**on (ona, ono) czyta**	**one (oni) czytają**
	he/she/it reads / is reading	*they read / are reading*

The titles **panowie** *gentlemen* and **panie** *ladies* may be used instead of **państwo** in second-person plural titled address. Relation names are often used in titled address as a form of respect.

Czy mama nie rozumie?   Doesn't Mother understand?

Lack of Auxiliary Verbs

Polish has no equivalent of the English auxiliary, or "helping," verbs *be, have, do,* and *used to.* In English, these verbs are used to make compound verb expressions of the sort *I am asking, I have been running, do you smoke,* and *we used to live.* In all such instances, Polish uses a single verb form. The nuance of the Polish verb is determined by context; thus, **pytam** can be interpreted as *I ask, I do ask, I am asking, I have been asking,* and **mieszkaliśmy** can be interpreted as *we lived, we were living, we used to live,* and *we had been living.*

Present Tense

The citation form of the verb (the dictionary form) is the infinitive. For each verb, one must also learn the first- and second-person singular forms of the present tense. The other forms of the present tense can be predicted from these two forms. There are four classes, or conjugations, of Polish verbs, based on the set of present tense endings; the class of a verb is evident from its first- and second-person singular forms.

Class 1 Verbs

Here are the endings for Class 1 verbs:

Class 1: Verbs in -ę -esz

	Singular	Plural
First-person	-ę	-emy
Second-person	-esz	-ecie
Third-person	-e	-ą

Here is an example of a Class 1 verb conjugated in the present tense:

chcieć *want*

chcę	I want	**chcemy**	we want
chcesz	you (*sg.*) want	**chcecie**	you (*pl.*) want
chce	he/she/it wants	**chcą**	they want

If there is a change in the stem between the first- and second-person forms, the third-person plural form uses the first-person singular stem; the other forms use the second-person singular stem. In other words, in order to predict the entire present tense conjugation from the first- and second-person singular forms, the third-person plural form is obtained by substituting ą for ę, and the other forms are obtained by substituting -e, -emy, -ecie for -esz. Here are some Class 1 verbs with a stem change in the present tense:

móc *can, be able*

mogę	I can	**możemy**	we can
możesz	you (*sg.*) can	**możecie**	you (*pl.*) can
może	he/she/it can	**mogą**	they can

brać *take*

biorę	I take	**bierzemy**	we take
bierzesz	you (*sg.*) take	**bierzecie**	you (*pl.*) take
bierze	he/she/it takes	**biorą**	they take

iść *go (on foot)*

idę	I go	**idziemy**	we go
idziesz	you (*sg.*) go	**idziecie**	you (*pl.*) go
idzie	he/she/it goes	**idą**	they go

In the present tense of **iść**, the stem alternates between **d** in the first-person singular and third-person plural forms and **dź** (spelled **dzi-**) in the other forms. Occasionally, there is a change in the root vowel in addition to a change in stem consonant.

nieść *carry*

niosę	I carry	**niesiemy**	we carry
niesiesz	you (*sg.*) carry	**niesiecie**	you (*pl.*) carry
niesie	he/she/it carries	**niosą**	they carry

Class 1 contains a relatively large number of subclasses, but these subclasses do not need to be learned as long as one learns the first- and second-person singular forms along with the infinitive.

Class 2 Verbs

Here are the endings for Class 2 verbs:

Class 2: Verbs in -ę -y/isz, infinitive in -y/ić or -eć

	Singular	Plural
First-person	**-ę**	**-y/imy**
Second-person	**-y/isz**	**-y/icie**
Third-person	**-y/i**	**-ą**

Here is an example of a Class 2 verb conjugated in the present tense:

lubić *like*

lubię	I like	**lubimy**	we like
lubisz	you (*sg.*) like	**lubicie**	you (*pl.*) like
lubi	he/she/it likes	**lubią**	they like

As with Class 1 verbs, if there is a change in the stem between the first- and second-person forms, the third-person plural form uses the first-person singular stem; the other forms use the second-person singular stem.

nosić *carry*

noszę	I carry	**nosimy**	we carry
nosisz	you (*sg.*) carry	**nosicie**	you (*pl.*) carry
nosi	he/she/it carries	**noszą**	they carry

In the present tense of **nosić**, the stem alternates between **sz** in the first-person singular and third-person plural forms and **ś** (spelled **si**) in the other forms.

lecieć *fly*

lecę	I fly	**lecimy**	we fly
lecisz	you (*sg.*) fly	**lecicie**	you (*pl.*) fly
leci	he/she/it flies	**lecą**	they fly

In the present tense of **lecieć**, the stem alternates between **c** in the first-person singular and third-person plural forms and **ć** (spelled **ci**) in the other forms. Verbs with the present tense in **-ę -ysz** do not have stem alternations.

uczyć *teach*

uczę	I teach	**uczymy**	we teach
uczysz	you (*sg.*) teach	**uczycie**	you (*pl.*) teach
uczy	he/she/it teaches	**uczą**	they teach

słyszeć *hear*

słyszę	I hear	**słyszymy**	we hear
słyszysz	you (*sg.*) hear	**słyszycie**	you (*pl.*) hear
słyszy	he/she/it hears	**słyszą**	they hear

The Class 2 subclasses, which are more superficially based than those in Class 1, mainly depend on whether the infinitive ends in **-y/ić** or **-eć** and on spelling differences.

Class 3 Verbs

Here are the endings for Class 3 verbs:

Class 3: Verbs in *-am -asz*, infinitive in *-ać*

	Singular	Plural
First-person	-am	-amy
Second-person	-asz	-acie
Third-person	-a	-ają

Here is an example of a Class 3 verb conjugated in the present tense:

czekać *wait*

czekam	I wait	**czekamy**	we wait
czekasz	you (*sg.*) wait	**czekacie**	you (*pl.*) wait
czeka	he/she/it waits	**czekają**	they wait

Here is the present tense conjugation of a Class 3 verb with an exceptional infinitive in **-eć**:

mieć *have*

mam	I have	**mamy**	we have
masz	you (*sg.*) have	**macie**	you (*pl.*) have
ma	he/she/it has	**mają**	they have

The verb **dać** *dam dasz* give (pf.) is irregular in the third-person plural: **dadzą**. Except for this verb, one may predict the present tense forms of Class 3 verbs from the first-person singular in **-am**. There are no subclasses of verbs in Class 3, either in structural terms or in spelling differences.

Class 4 Verbs

Here are the endings for Class 4 verbs:

Class 4: Verbs in *-em -esz*

	Singular	Plural
First-person	**-em**	**-emy**
Second-person	**-esz**	**-ecie**
Third-person	**-e**	**-ejᶏ**

Here is an example of a Class 4 verb conjugated in the present tense:

umieć *know how*

umiem	I know how	**umiemy**	we know how
umiesz	you (*sg.*) know how	**umiecie**	you (*pl.*) know how
umie	he/she/it knows how	**umieją**	they know how

There are very few Class 4 verbs. As with Class 3 verbs, the forms of Class 4 verbs may be predicted from the first-person singular form, here in **-em**, and there are no subclasses. The endings of Class 3 and Class 4 verbs are the same, except for the vowel of the ending: **a** for Class 3, **e** for Class 4. The following three Class 4 verbs are irregular in the third-person plural form: They have **dz** instead of **j**.

wiedzieć *know (information)*

wiem	**wiemy**
wiesz	**wiecie**
wie	**wiedzą**

powiedzieć pf. *say*

powiem	powiemy
powiesz	powiecie
powie	powiedzą

jeść *eat*

jem	jemy
jesz	jecie
je	jedzą

Irregular Verb *być* be

The verb **być** *be* is irregular in the present tense:

być *be*

jestem	I am	jesteśmy	we are
jesteś	you (*sg.*) are	jesteście	you (*pl.*) are
jest	he/she/it is	są	they are

Być is the only verb with a simple (one-word) future tense.

będę	I will be	będziemy	we will be
będziesz	you (*sg.*) will be	będziecie	you (*pl.*) will be
będzie	he/she/it will be	będą	they will be

Imperative

Formation of the Imperative

The second-person singular informal imperative, or command, form of a verb is usually equivalent to the stem of the third-person singular present tense form of the verb; it is obtained by dropping **-e**, **-ie**, **-y**, or **-i** or by adding **j** to **-a**:

Infinitive	Present Tense Singular	Imperative
pisać	piszę, piszesz, pisze	pisz *write!*
iść	idę, idziesz, idzie	idź *go!*
kończyć	kończę, kończysz, kończy	kończ *finish!*
kupić	kupię, kupisz, kupi	kup *buy!*
czekać	czekam, czekasz, czeka	czekaj *wait!*

Occasionally, there is an **o** → **ó** vowel shift in the imperative stem.

robić	robię, robisz, robi	rób *do!*
otworzyć	otworzę, otworzysz, otworzy	otwórz *open!*

but

| chodzić | chodzę, chodzisz, chodzi | **chodź** *come!* |

Verbs whose stem ends in a consonant + **n** or **rz** add **-y/ij** to form the imperative.

| ciągnąć | ciągnę, ciągniesz, ciągnie | **ciągnij** *pull!* |
| zetrzeć | zetrę, zetrzesz, zetrze | **zetrzyj** *wipe off!* |

Verbs in **-awać** *-aję -ajesz* have exceptional imperative forms, which end in **-awaj**: **wstawać** *wstaję* imp. *wstawaj get up.* The following verbs also have exceptional imperative forms.

być	jestem, jesteś, jest, jesteśmy, jesteście, są	**bądź** *be!*
jeść	jem, jesz, je, 3pl. jedzą	**jedz** *eat!*
posłać	poślę, poślesz, pośle	**poślij** *send!*
powiedzieć	powiem, powiesz, powie	**powiedz** *say!*
rozumieć	rozumiem, rozumiesz, rozumie	**rozum** *understand!*
wziąć	wezmę, weźmiesz, weźmie	**weź** *take!*

The forms above are singular and informal, that is, they are used with close acquaintances and family members. The plural informal imperative is formed from the singular form by adding **-cie**: **idźcie** *go!* (pl.). The first-person plural form of exhortation is formed from the singular form by adding **-my**: **czekajmy** *let's wait!*, **chodźmy** *let's go!*

The formal imperative is formed with the particle **niech** *let* plus the third-person present tense form of the verb.

Niech pani usiądzie.	Why doesn't Madam sit down?
Niech pan się nie śmieje.	Don't laugh, sir!
Niech państwo wejdą.	Come on in, people.

The imperative, whether formal or informal, is often accompanied by the word **proszę** *please.*

| **Proszę wejdź.** | Please come in. |
| **Proszę niech pan poczeka.** | Please wait a moment, sir. |

Positive commands usually occur in the perfective aspect, while negative commands occur in the imperfective.

| **Otwórz okno.** (pf.) | Open the window. |
| **Nie otwieraj okna.** (impf.) | Don't open the window. |

A negated perfective imperative is likely to be considered a warning.

| **Nie otwórz drzwi!** | Watch out, don't open the door! |

The Pragmatic Imperative System

The system of actual pragmatic implementation of the imperative differs from what is given in the formal charts above. Because of the use of the hortatory particle **niech** with third-person pronouns of polite address, and occasionally with first-person pronouns, the pragmatic system can be considered to consist of eight forms instead of only three.

Formal System

	Singular	Plural
First-person	—	**napiszmy**
		let's write
Second-person	**napisz**	**napiszcie**
	write!	*write!*
Third-person	—	—

Pragmatic System

	Singular	Plural
First-person	**niech napiszę**	**napiszmy**
	why don't I write	*let's write*
Second-person informal	**napisz**	**napiszcie**
	write!	*write!*
Second-person formal	**niech pan napisze**	**niech państwo napiszą**
	why don't you write, sir	*why don't you write, ladies and gentlemen*
Third-person	**niech on napisze**	**niech oni napiszą**
	why doesn't he write	*why don't they write*

The first-person singular use with **niech** is not common. As the chart suggests, constructions using **niech** often translate into English as *why don't....*

Niech ja to zrobię.	Why don't *I* do that?
Niech pani to kupi.	Why don't you buy that, Madam?

Past Tense

The past tense of Polish verbs is formed from the infinitive stem. There is no verb-class distinction in the past tense, unlike in the present tense. The rules for forming the past tense differ slightly, according to whether the infinitive ends (a) in a vowel plus ć (for example, **czytać** *read,* **umieć** *know how,* **lubić** *like,* **uczyć** *teach,* **psuć** *spoil,* and **ciąć** *cut*) or (b) in -ść, -źć, or -c (for example, **nieść** *carry,* **leźć** *crawl,* and **piec** *bake*).

For verbs with infinitives ending in a vowel plus ć, the third-person forms are created by removing the final -ć and adding -ł (masculine), -ła (feminine), **-ło** (neuter), **-li** (masculine personal plural), or **-ły** (other plural). The first- and second-person forms are created from the third-person by adding personal endings to them. The past tense personal endings, which are similar to the present tense endings of **być** *be,* are as follows:

	Singular	Plural
First-person	**-m**	**-śmy**
Second-person	**-ś**	**-ście**
Third-person	—	—

With masculine forms, the linking vowel **e** is added before **-m** and **-ś**, creating the endings **-em** and **-eś**.

Here is the conjugation of **dać** *give* in the past tense:

Singular
dałem (masc.) *I gave*   **dałam** (fem.) *I gave*
dałeś (masc.) *you* (sg.) *gave*   **dałaś** (fem.) *you* (sg.) *gave*
dał *he gave*   **dała** *she gave*   **dało** *it gave* (neut.)

Plural
daliśmy (masc.pers.) *we gave*   **dałyśmy** (fem.) *we gave*
daliście (masc.pers.) *you* (pl.) *gave*   **dałyście** (fem.) *you* (pl.) *gave*
dali (masc.pers.) *they gave*   **dały** (fem./neut.) *they gave*

Verbs with infinitives in **-eć** change **e** to **a** in all forms except the masculine personal plural.

mieć *have*
Singular
miałem (masc.) *I had*   **miałam** (fem.) *I had*
miałeś (masc.) *you had*   **miałaś** (fem.) *you had*
miał *he had*   **miała** *she had*   **miało** *it had* (neut.)

Plural
mieliśmy (masc.pers.) *we had*   **miałyśmy** (fem.) *we had*
mieliście (masc.pers.) *you had*   **miałyście** (fem.) *you had*
mieli (masc.pers.) *they had*   **miały** (fem./neut.) *they had*

Verbs with infinitives in **-ąć** change **ą** to **ę** in all forms except the masculine singular.

zacząć *begin*

Singular

zacząłem (masc.) *I began*	**zaczęłam** (fem.) *I began*	
zacząłeś (masc.) *you began*	**zaczęłaś** (fem.) *you began*	
zaczął *he began*	**zaczęła** *she began*	**zaczęło** *it began* (neut.)

Plural

zaczęliśmy (masc.pers.) *we began*	**zaczęłyśmy** (fem.) *we began*	
zaczęliście (masc.pers.) *you began*	**zaczęłyście** (fem.) *you began*	
zaczęli (masc.pers.) *they began*	**zaczęły** (fem./neut.) *they began*	

Verbs with infinitives in **-ść**, **-źć**, and **-c** add past tense endings to stems similar to those found in the first-person singular present tense.

nieść niosę niesiesz *carry*

Singular

niosłem (masc.) *I carried*	**niosłam** (fem.) *I carried*	
niosłeś (masc.) *you carried*	**niosłaś** (fem.) *you carried*	
niósł *he carried*	**niosła** *she carried*	**niosło** *it carried* (neut.)

Plural

nieśliśmy (masc.pers.) *we carried*	**niosłyśmy** (fem.) *we carried*	
nieśliście (masc.pers.) *you carried*	**niosłyście** (fem.) *you carried*	
nieśli (masc.pers.) *they carried*	**niosły** (fem./neut.) *they carried*	

móc mogę możesz *can, be able*

Singular

mogłem (masc.) *I could*	**mogłam** (fem.) *I could*	
mogłeś (masc.) *you could*	**mogłaś** (fem.) *you could*	
mógł *he could*	**mogła** *she could*	**mogło** *it could* (neut.)

Plural

mogliśmy (masc.pers.) *we could*	**mogłyśmy** (fem.) *we could*	
mogliście (masc.pers.) *you could*	**mogłyście** (fem.) *you could*	
mogli (masc.pers.) *they could*	**mogły** (fem./neut.) *they could*	

With **nieść** and **móc**, the **o** of the stem becomes **ó** in the third-person singular masculine. With **nieść**, the **o** of the stem becomes **e** in the masculine personal plural.

The following verbs have irregular past tense formations.

	Third-Person Past Tense
iść *idę idziesz* go (det.)	(sg.) **szedł, szła, szło**
	(pl.) **szli, szły**
jeść *jem jesz* 3pl. *jedzą* eat	(sg.) **jadł, jadła, jadło**
	(pl.) **jedli, jadły**
usiąść *usiądę usiądziesz* sit down (pf.)	(sg.) **usiadł, usiadła, usiadło**
	(pl.) **usiedli, usiadły**
znaleźć *znajdę znajdziesz* find (pf.)	(sg.) **znalazł, znalazła, znalazło**
	(pl.) **znaleźli, znalazły**

Compound Future Tense

The compound future tense is formed only with imperfective verbs. The auxiliary verb **będę, będziesz, będzie, będziemy, będziecie, będą** is used, plus the third-person past tense form. Here is the conjugation of **czytać** *read* in the future tense:

Singular

będę czytał (masc.)	**będę czytała** (fem.)	
I am going to read	*I am going to read*	
będziesz czytał (masc.)	**będziesz czytała** (fem.)	
you are going to read	*you are going to read*	
będzie czytał (masc.)	**będzie czytała** (fem.)	**będzie czytało** (neut.)
he is going to read	*she is going to read*	*it* (e.g., **dziecko** *child*) *is going to read*

Plural

będziemy czytali (masc.pers.)	**będziemy czytały** (fem.)
we are going to read	*we are going to read*
będziecie czytali (masc.pers.)	**będziecie czytały** (fem.)
you are going to read	*you are going to read*
oni będą czytali (masc.pers.)	**one będą czytały** (fem.)
they are going to read	*they are going to read*

Instead of the third-person past tense form, the infinitive may be used, for example, **będę czytać** *I am going to read*. The use of the past tense form is slightly more colloquial but is, in any case, practically obligatory with males.

Perfective and Imperfective Aspect

Polish verbs can be either perfective or imperfective, and most verbal notions are expressed by a pair of verbs, one of which is imperfective (impf.) and the other perfective (pf.). Usually, the members of these aspect pairs are transparently related, but sometimes they are not, as in the case of **brać** *biorę bierzesz* impf., pf. **wziąć** *wezmę weźmiesz take.* The future tense construction with **będę**, etc. is used only with imperfective verbs. With perfective verbs, which have no present tense meaning, the present tense form by itself generally expresses future meaning. For example, the verb **kupić** *buy* is perfective, so its present forms have future meaning.

kupię *I will buy*   **kupimy** *we will buy*
kupisz *you* (sg.) *will buy*   **kupicie** *you* (pl.) *will buy*
kupi *he/she/it will buy*   **kupią** *they will buy*

Perfective verbs have a related imperfective verb in order to express present meaning. Corresponding to the perfective verb **kupić** *buy* is the imperfective verb **kupować**, whose present tense forms follow:

kupuję *I buy / am buying*   **kupujemy** *we buy / are buying*
kupujesz *you* (sg.) *buy / are buying*   **kupujecie** *you* (pl.) *buy / are buying*
kupuje *he/she/it buys / is buying*   **kupują** *they buy / are buying*

Perfective verbs are often formed from imperfective verbs by adding a prefix. Here are some common imperfective verbs with their primary perfective prefix:

Imperfective	Primary Perfective
budować *build*	**zbudować**
chcieć *want*	**zechcieć**
cieszyć się *be glad*	**ucieszyć się**
czekać *wait*	**zaczekać**
czytać *read*	**przeczytać**
dziękować *thank*	**podziękować**
dziwić się *be surprised*	**zdziwić się**
gotować *prepare*	**przygotować**
gotować *cook*	**ugotować**
grać *play*	**zagrać**
iść/chodzić *go (on foot)*	**pójść**
jechać/jeździć *go, ride*	**pojechać**
jeść *eat*	**zjeść**
kończyć *finish*	**skończyć**
lecieć *fly*	**polecieć**
leżeć *lie*	**poleżeć**
myć się *wash (oneself)*	**umyć się**

Imperfective	Primary Perfective
mylić się *err*	**pomylić się**
nieść/nosić *carry*	**odnieść**
pić *drink*	**wypić**
pisać *write*	**napisać**
płacić *pay*	**zapłacić**
płakać *cry*	**zapłakać**
pytać *ask*	**zapytać**
robić *do*	**zrobić**
rozumieć *understand*	**zrozumieć**
siedzieć *sit*	**posiedzieć**
słyszeć *hear*	**usłyszeć**
śmiać się *laugh*	**zaśmiać się**
śpiewać *sing*	**zaśpiewać**
tańczyć *dance*	**zatańczyć**

Sometimes, when there is felt to be no logical perfective notion corresponding to the unprefixed imperfective, prefixation slightly alters the meaning of the word: **żyć** *live,* pf. **przeżyć** *live through, survive*; **grać** *play,* pf. **zagrać** *begin to play,* pf. **pograć** *play a little.* Often, however, perfective prefixation is used both to form a perfective verb and to create a verb with a new (and often unpredictable) meaning: **wygrać** *win* and **przegrać** *lose* are both based on **grać** *play.*

Imperfective verbs are typically formed from prefixed perfective verbs in new meanings (as, for example, **przegrać** *lose* is a "new meaning" from **grać** *play*) by adding a stem extension and, usually, by changing the conjugation type, usually to Class 3, but sometimes to Class 1. Here are some examples:

Perfective	Derived Imperfective
dać *dam dasz* 3pl. *dadzą give*	**dawać** *daję dajesz*
otworzyć *-rzę -rzysz open*	**otwierać** *-am -asz*
pokazać *-żę -żesz show*	**pokazywać** *-zuję -zujesz*
pomóc *-mogę -możesz help*	**pomagać** *-am -asz*
poznać *-am -asz meet*	**poznawać** *-znaję -znajesz*
przypomnieć *-mnę -mnisz remind*	**przypominać** *-am -asz*
spotkać *-am -asz meet*	**spotykać** *-am -asz*
ubrać się *ubiorę ubierzesz dress*	**ubierać się** *-am -asz*
użyć *-yję -yjesz use*	**używać** *-am -asz*
wygrać *-am -asz win*	**wygrywać** *-am -asz*
zacząć *-cznę -czniesz start*	**zaczynać** *-am -asz*
zamknąć *-nę -niesz close, shut*	**zamykać** *-am -asz*
zamówić *-wię -wisz order*	**zamawiać** *-am -asz*
zaprosić *-szę -sisz invite*	**zapraszać** *-am -asz*
zdarzyć się *zdarzy* (3sg.) *happen*	**zdarzać się** *zdarza*

Perfective	Derived Imperfective
zdjąć *zdejmę zdejmiesz take off*	zdejmować *-muję -mujesz*
zostawić *-wię -wisz leave behind*	zostawiać *-am -asz*

A few verbs have highly irregular, or even etymologically unrelated as-pect partners.

Imperfective	Perfective
brać *biorę bierzesz take*	wziąć *wezmę weźmiesz*
kłaść *kładę kładziesz put, place, lay*	położyć *-żę -żysz*
kupować *-puję -pujesz buy*	kupić *-pię -pisz*
mówić *-wię -wisz say, speak, talk*	powiedzieć *-wiem -wiesz*
	3pl. *-wiedzą*
oglądać *-am -asz watch*	obejrzeć *-rzę -rzysz*
widzieć *-dzę -dzisz see*	zobaczyć *-czę -czysz*
wkładać *-am -asz put on*	włożyć *-żę -żysz*
znajdować *-duję -dujesz*	znaleźć *znajdę znajdziesz find*

For more examples, see the verb list in Chapter 11.

Summary: The Polish Tense-Aspect System

	Imperfective	Perfective
Present	robię *I do / am doing*	—
Past	robiłem *I did / was doing* (masc.)	zrobiłem *I did / got done*
Future	będę robił *I will do / be doing*	zrobię *I'll do / get done*

Verbs of Motion

Polish distinguishes between movement on foot and movement by vehicle. In either case, the simple verbs for motion distinguish ongoing (determinate (det.)) activity from frequentative (indeterminate (indet.)) activity. This dis-tinction applies only to the imperfective aspect. Here are the most important motion verbs:

	Determinate	Indeterminate
go on foot	iść *idę idziesz*	chodzić *-dzę -dzisz*
go by vehicle	jechać *jadę jedziesz*	jeździć *jeżdżę jeździsz*
carry on foot	nieść *niosę niesiesz*	nosić *noszę nosisz*
carry by vehicle	wieźć *wiozę wieziesz*	wozić *wożę wozisz*
run	biec *biegnę biegniesz*	biegać *-am -asz*
fly, rush	lecieć *-cę -cisz*	latać *-am -asz*
sail, swim	płynąć *-nę -niesz*	pływać *-am -asz*

Gdzie teraz idziesz?	Where are you going now?
Czy często chodzisz do kina?	Do you go to the movies often?

| **Jadę do Warszawy pociągiem.** | I'm going to Warsaw by train. |
| **Zwykle jeżdżę do Warszawy pociągiem.** | I usually travel to Warsaw by train. |

| **Przepraszam, ale muszę lecieć.** | Excuse me, but I have to run. |
| **Nie lubię latać.** | I don't like to fly. |

When perfectively prefixed, verbs of motion lose the determinate vs. indeterminate distinction. The determinate and indeterminate forms have a single prefixed perfective partner, formed on the determinate verb. Here are the prefixed perfectives of the verbs above; most are formed with **po-**:

	Imperfective	**Perfective**
go on foot	**iść, chodzić**	**pójść**
go by vehicle	**jechać, jeździć**	**pojechać**
carry on foot	**nieść, nosić**	**zanieść, odnieść, ponieść**
carry by vehicle	**wieźć, wozić**	**zawieźć, odwieźć, powieźć**
run	**biec, biegać**	**pobiec**
fly, rush	**lecieć, latać**	**polecieć**
sail, swim	**płynąć, pływać**	**popłynąć**

Here are the most common prefixed perfective forms of **iść** and **jechać** and their derived imperfective aspect partners:

	Perfective	**Imperfective**
arrive, come on foot	**przyjść**	**przychodzić**
leave on foot	**wyjść**	**wychodzić**
go away from	**odejść**	**odchodzić**
approach, come up to	**podejść**	**podchodzić**
arrive by vehicle	**przyjechać**	**przyjeżdżać**
leave by vehicle	**wyjechać**	**wyjeżdżać**
drive away from	**odjechać**	**odjeżdżać**
approach, come up to	**podjechać**	**podjeżdżać**

Conditional Mood

The conditional mood is used to express conditional or suppositional ideas that, in English, are typically expressed by *would, could, should,* and *might.* The conditional is also used in contrary-to-fact statements and is required in indirect commands and requests.

The conditional is formed by using the third-person past tense forms of the verb, plus the conditional particle **by** (which is either attached to the verb stem or, preferably, to some intonationally minor item occurring earlier in the sentence), plus personal endings. Here is the conditional conjugation of **pomóc** *-mogę -możesz help* (pf.):

Singular

	Masc.	Fem.
First-person	**pomógłbym**	**pomogłabym**
	I would help	*I would help*
Second-person	**pomógłbyś**	**pomogłabyś**
	you would help	*you would help*
Third-person	**pomógłby**	**pomogłaby**
	he would help	*she would help*

Plural

	Masc.Pers.	Other
First-person	**pomoglibyśmy**	**pomogłybyśmy**
	we would help	*we would help*
Second-person	**pomoglibyście**	**pomogłybyście**
	you would help	*you would help*
Third-person	**pomogliby**	**pomogłyby**
	they would help	*they would help*

If **by** is attached to another word, it is usually to a subordinating conjunction like **że** *that* or **gdy** *if*:

Singular

	Masc.	Fem.
First-person	**gdybym pomógł**	**gdybym pomogła**
	if I would help	*if I would help*
Second-person	**gdybyś pomógł**	**gdybyś pomogła**
	if you would help	*if you would help*
Third-person	**gdyby pomógł**	**gdyby pomogła**
	if he would help	*if she would help*

Plural

	Masc.Pers.	Other
First-person	**gdybyśmy pomogli**	**gdybyśmy pomogły**
	if we would help	*if we would help*
Second-person	**gdybyście pomogli**	**gdybyście pomogły**
	if you would help	*if you would help*
Third-person	**gdyby pomogli**	**gdyby pomogły**
	if they would help	*if they would help*

The conditional is primarily used:

1. In clauses of purpose

Powtórzę to jeszcze raz, żebyś to dobrze zrozumiała.	I'll repeat that one more time, so that you understand it correctly.

When the subjects of both clauses refer to the same person or thing, the infinitive is used instead:

Muszę wrócić do biblioteki,   I have to go back to the library to
żeby oddać książkę.   return a book.

After verbs of motion, the infinitive is more often used by itself, without **żeby**:

Idę na pocztę kupić znaczki.   I'm going to the post office to buy
                                          stamps.

2. In contrary-to-fact clauses

Pomogłabym ci, gdybym nie   I would help you, if I were not so busy.
była tak zajęta.

Although a past contrary-to-fact conditional can theoretically be formed by adding the third-person past tense form of **być**, as in **gdybyśmy pomogli byli** *if we had helped,* in practice the regular conditional tense can have either future or past reference.

3. After verbs of request, command, proposal, and desire

Proszę was, żebyście nie robili   I'm asking that you not make such
takiego hałasu.   a racket.

4. To express hypothetical possibilities

Czy mógłbyś mi pomóc?   Could you help me?

5. To express vague speculations and suppositions

Nie sądzę, żeby on był teraz   I don't think he would be at home now.
w domu.

Gerunds, Participles, and Verbal Nouns

Polish has a well-developed system of verbal adverbs (gerunds), verbal adjectives (participles), and verbal nouns, in both perfective and imperfective aspects. The sample verb in the chart below is **pisać** *piszę piszesz* impf., pf. **napisać** *write.*

	Imperfective	Perfective
Gerund	**pisząc** *while writing*	**napisawszy** *having written*
Active participle	**piszący** *(who is) writing*	—
Passive participle	**pisany** *written* (impf.)	**napisany** *written* (pf.)
Verbal noun	**pisanie** *the writing* (impf.)	**napisanie** *the writing* (pf.)

Gerunds

A gerund is a verb form without personal endings; the person of the verb is inferred from context. The imperfective gerund can often be translated as *while doing something*: **pisząc** *while writing*. The perfective gerund usually means *after having done something*: **napisawszy** *after having written*. Gerunds are used to incorporate one sentence into another when the subject of both sentences is the same.

Czytając gazetę, palił fajkę.	While reading the paper, he smoked a pipe.
Zjadłszy kolację, on wstał i wyszedł.	Having finished supper, he stood up and left.

Imperfective Gerund

The imperfective gerund is formed by adding **-c** to the third-person plural present tense form of an imperfective verb: **czytają**, gerund **czytając** *while reading*; **idą**, gerund **idąc** *while going*.

Perfective Gerund

The perfective gerund is formed from the third-person masculine singular past tense form of a perfective verb. If the form ends in a vowel + **-ł**, the **-ł** is replaced by **-wszy**: **przeczytał**, gerund **przeczytawszy** *having read*; **zrobił**, gerund **zrobiwszy** *having done*. If the form ends in a consonant + **ł**, **-szy** is added: **wyszedł**, gerund **wyszedłszy** *having left*; **wyniósł**, gerund **wyniósłszy** *having carried out*. The perfective gerund is going out of use and is hardly ever used in speech.

Participles

A participle is an adjective derived from a verb. It retains many of the properties of the verb, for example, aspect and the ability to take a complement. The imperfective active participle is often translated as a relative clause (*who/what is doing*), and it is often separated from the noun it modifies by its complement.

Czytający gazetę człowiek nic nie zauważył.	The man reading the paper noticed nothing.

Like other adjectives, participles have a complete set of gender, case, and number endings.

Imperfective Active Participle

The imperfective active participle is formed by adding adjective endings to the imperfective gerund: **czytając**, participle *czytający czytająca czytające*

masc.pers.pl. *czytający who is reading*; **idąc**, participle *idący idąca idące*
masc.pers.pl. *idący who is going*.

Passive Participle

A passive participle describes an object on which an action has been carried
out. The imperfective passive participle **czytany** means *being read*. The
perfective passive participle **przeczytany** means *having been read*. The latter is more frequently used, often in a construction with the verb **zostać**:

Ta książka została już przeczytana.	That book has already been read.

See Passive Voice below.

The passive participle is usually formed from the infinitive stem, as
follows:

1. Verbs with infinitives in **-ać** and **-eć** form the passive participle in **-any**
-ana -ane -ani: **napisać** *write*, participle *napisany napisana napisane*
masc.pers.pl. *napisani written*; **widzieć** *see*, participle *widziany widziana*
widziane masc.pers.pl. *widziani seen*.

2. Verbs with infinitives in **-ić** and **-yć** form the passive participle in **-ony**
-ona -one -eni, added to a stem like that of the first-person singular present tense: **zawstydzić** *-dzę -dzisz* embarrass, participle *zawstydzony za-*
wstydzona zawstydzone masc.pers.pl. *zawstydzeni embarrassed*. Monosyl-
labic verbs in **-ić** and **-yć**, like **pić** *drink*, **myć** *wash*, and their derivatives,
like **wypić** *drink* and **umyć** *wash*, do not follow this rule; see No. 4 below.

3. Verbs with infinitives in **-ść**, **-źć**, and **-c** form the passive participle in
-ony -ona -one -eni, added to a stem like that of the second-person singular
present tense: **wynieść** *-niosę -niesiesz carry out*, participle *wyniesiony*
wyniesiona wyniesione masc.pers.pl. *wyniesieni carried out*; **przegryźć**
-zę -ziesz bite through, participle *przegryziony przegryziona przegryzione*
masc.pers.pl. *przegryzieni bitten through*; **upiec upiekę upieczesz** *bake*,
participle *upieczony upieczona upieczone* masc.pers.pl. *upieczeni baked*.
An irregular past participle in this group is **znaleźć znajdę znajdziesz** *find*,
participle *znaleziony znaleziona znalezione* masc.pers.pl. *znalezieni found*.
Stems in **ć (ci)** and **dź (dzi)** show **c** and **dz**, respectively, in the masculine
personal plural: **zgnieść zgniotę zgnieciesz** *crush*, participle *zgnieciony*
zgnieciona zgniecione masc.pers.pl. *zgnieceni crushed*; **zawieść zawiodę**
zawiedziesz *lead astray*, participle *zawiedziony zawiedziona zawiedzione*
masc.pers.pl. *zawiedzeni led astray*.

4. Verbs with infinitives in vowels other than **a** and **e** plus **ć**, and monosyl-
labic verbs in **-ić** and **-yć** form the passive participle by dropping **ć** and add-

ing -ty -ta -te -ci: zepsuć *-uję -ujesz spoil,* participle *zepsuty zepsuta zepsute* masc.pers.pl. *zepsuci spoiled*; użyć *-yję -yjesz use,* participle *użyty użyta użyte* masc.pers.pl. *użyci used.*

Verbs in **-nąć** form the passive participle by dropping **nąć** and adding **-nięty -nięta -nięte -nięci**: zamknąć *-nę -niesz lock, shut, close,* participle *zamknięty zamknięta zamknięte* masc.pers.pl. *zamknięci locked, shut, closed.* Other verbs in **-ąć** form the passive participle by dropping **ąć** and adding **-ęty -ęta -ęte -ęci**: zacząć *-cznę -czniesz begin,* participle *zaczęty zaczęta zaczęte* masc.pers.pl. *zaczęci begun.*

Verbal Nouns

A verbal noun is a noun derived from a verb that still retains many of the properties of the verb, including aspect. Both **czytanie** and **przeczytanie** are usually translated as *reading,* the first referring to the action, the second to the accomplishment. Verbal nouns often occur with the prepositions **przy** *while, during,* **przed** *before,* and **po** *after.* They are often followed by a noun in the genitive case.

Po przeczytaniu tej książki   After reading that book, I'll go to bed.
pójdę spać.

Verbal nouns also often occur in phrases following the preposition **do**: **woda do picia** *drinking water,* **nic do zrobienia** *nothing to do.*

The verbal noun is formed on a stem like that of the masculine personal plural of the passive participle; thus, participles in **-ony** form the verbal noun in **-enie**: participle **podniesiony** masc.pers.pl. **podniesieni**, verbal noun **podniesienie** *elevation.* Participles in **-ty** form the verbal noun in **-cie**: participle **zatruty** masc.pers.pl. **zatruci**, verbal noun **zatrucie** *poisoning.*

Gerunds and participles formed from verbs with **się** retain **się**, while verbal nouns formed from verbs with **się** sometimes lose the **się**: **golić się** *shave oneself,* participle **goląc się** *while shaving oneself,* and usually **golenie** *shaving* (although **golenie się** is not wrong).

Some verbs rarely form the verbal noun; an independent noun is used instead. For example, **obawa** *fear* is the de facto verbal noun of **bać się** *be afraid* and **obawiać się** *fear.*

Passive Voice

An active, transitive sentence (a sentence with a subject, verb, and direct object) can be transformed into the passive voice, using a passive participle, which presents the action from the point of view of the direct object. Compare the English sentences *John is frying an egg* (active) and *An egg is being fried by John* (passive). In the second sentence, *fried* is the passive participle, linked to the object by the verb *be*. In Polish, the linking verb is **być** *be* with imperfective verbs, and **zostać** *zostanę zostaniesz become* with perfective verbs.

	Active	Passive
Imperfective		
Present	**Jan czyta książkę.**	**Książka jest czytana przez Jana.**
	Jan is reading the book.	*The book is being read by Jan.*
Past	**Jan czytał książkę.**	**Książka była czytana przez Jana.**
	Jan was reading the book.	*The book was being read by Jan.*
Future	**Jan będzie czytał książkę.**	**Książka będzie czytana przez Jana.**
	Jan is going to read the book.	*The book is going to be read by Jan.*

Perfective		
Past	**Jan przeczytał książkę.**	**Książka została przeczytana przez Jana.**
	Jan read the book.	*The book was read by Jan.*
Future	**Jan przeczyta książkę.**	**Książka zostanie przeczytana przez Jana.**
	Jan will read the book.	*The book will be read by Jan.*

The original subject may be preserved by placing its accusative form after the preposition **przez**: **przez Jana** *by Jan*. If the original subject was a force of nature, it may be placed in the instrumental with no preposition.

Drzewo zostało obalone wiatrem.   The tree was knocked down by the wind.

The practical effect of the passive voice is often achieved by simply reversing the order of the subject and object in an active sentence. For example, **Książkę czyta Jan** *book* (acc.) *reads Jan* (nom.) has about the same effect as **Książka jest czytana przez Jana.** *The book is read by Jan.*

Depersonal Verbs

There is a difference in Polish between a verb with a definite subject that is simply not expressed and a verb that has no subject to begin with; the latter is called a depersonal verb. The Polish depersonal verb system is well developed. For the most part, it is based on the third-person singular neuter form of the finite verb, with the particle **się** functioning as the de facto subject.

	Imperfective	Perfective
Present		
one reads	**czyta się**	—
Past		
one read,	**czytało się** OR **czytano**	**przeczytało się** OR
one used to read		**przeczytano**
Future		
one will read	**będzie się czytało**	**przeczyta się**

The construction **czyta się** means *one reads* or *reading is going on*. A form like this may take a direct object, just as a personal verb does.

Czyta się książkę.	One reads a book.
	OR A book is being read.

In the past tense, the form based on **się** is usually replaced with a form based on the passive participle stem plus the ending **-o**.

Czytano książki.	One read books.
	OR Books were being read.

Reflexive Verbs

In a broad sense, reflexive verbs are verbs that occur with the reflexive particle **się**. In colloquial speech, the particle **się** tends to occur before the verb; however, it can never occur in initial position in a clause.

Bardzo się śpieszę.	I'm in a big hurry.

but

Śpieszę się.	I'm in a hurry.

Following are the most important functions of the particle **się**.

Literal Reflexive Use

The basic meaning of the reflexive particle **się** is *oneself* in literal reflexive uses (where the actor performs an action on himself). This is not necessarily the most frequent use of this particle, but it is the one on which most other uses are based. Frequently encountered are verbs of personal grooming.

czesać (się) *czeszę czeszesz*	comb (one's hair)
kąpać (się) *kąpię kąpiesz*	bathe (oneself)
myć (się) *myję myjesz*	wash (oneself)
golić (się) *golę golisz*	shave (oneself)

Compare the following two sentences.

Muszę umyć ręce.	I have to wash my hands. (*transitive without* **się**)
Muszę się umyć.	I have to wash up. (*reflexive with* **się**)

For pragmatic reasons, verbs of this type, that is, verbs of personal grooming, occur with **się** more often than not.

Codziennie się kąpię.	I take a bath every day.
Golę się przed śniadaniem.	I shave before breakfast.

Reciprocal Use

The reflexive particle **się** can be used with a verb whose action can be considered reciprocal (back and forth). In this case, the particle **się** takes on the sense "each other / one another."

Dobrze się znamy.	We know each other well.
Bardzo się lubimy/kochamy.	We like/love each other a lot.
Często się spotykamy.	We meet one another often.

The verb must be able to have an accusative object for the **się** reciprocal construction to be possible. Otherwise, the appropriate case form of the reflexive pronoun is used. For example, since **pomagać** *-am -asz help* takes the dative case, *help one another* is expressed with the dative reflexive, **sobie.**

Często sobie pomagamy.	We often help one another.

Intransitivization

Polish is sensitive to whether a verb is used transitively (with a direct object) or intransitively (without a direct object). If a verb can be used transitively in its basic sense, its intransitive counterpart is formed with **się**. Three subtypes of this use may be distinguished, consisting of uses with persons, things, and events.

1. Use with persons

Transitive	**Intransitive**
nazywać *-am -asz call, name*	**nazywać się** *be called*
śpieszyć *-szę -szysz hurry (someone)*	**śpieszyć się** *be in a hurry*
Jak oni nazywają swoją żaglówkę?	What do they call their sailboat?
Jak ich żaglówka się nazywa?	What's their sailboat called?

2. Use with things

Transitive	Intransitive
otwierać *-am -asz* open	otwierać się
zamykać *-am -asz* close	zamykać się

Zamykamy książki.	We are closing our books.
Drzwi się zamykają.	The door is closing.

3. Use with events

Transitive	Intransitive
zaczynać *-am -asz* begin	zaczynać się
kończyć *-czę -czysz* end, finish	kończyć się

Zaczynamy/kończymy lekcję.	We are beginning/ending the lesson.
Lekcja się zaczyna/kończy.	The lesson is beginning/ending.

Depersonalization

With the third-person singular form of a verb, the particle **się** can express the idea of the impersonal *one,* as though it were the subject of the sentence. This use is frequent, much more so than the corresponding use of *one* in English.

Jak to się mówi/pisze?	How does one say/write that?
Jak tam się idzie/jedzie?	How does one go there?
Tam zawsze długo się czeka.	One always waits a long time there.

Depersonal verbs may take an accusative direct object in the same way as other verbs.

Kiedy się ma temperaturę, trzeba zostać w domu.	When one has a temperature, one should stay at home.

A sentence can be depersonalized by adding **się** and placing the subject in the dative case.

Przyjemnie mi się z tobą rozmawia.	It's pleasant talking with you.

In English, the second-person singular form of a verb is often used impersonally, as in *How do you say that?* Comparable use in Polish should be avoided, since it is likely to be taken for informal speech. It is safer to express the question *How do you get to Lodz?* with a depersonal verb: **Jak się jedzie do Łodzi?** OR **Jak można dostać się do Łodzi?**

Impersonal Verbs

The particle **się** is used with certain verbs to make them impersonal, where English uses *it* as the subject of an impersonal verb.

wydawać się *wydaje* (+ dat.)	it seems
chcieć się *chce* (+ dat.)	it feels like (to me), (I) feel like
rozumieć się *rozumie*	it is understood

Such verbs often take dative complements.

Wydaje mi się, że skądś znam tę panią.	It seems to me I know that lady from somewhere.
Nie chce mi się iść do miasta.	I don't feel like going to town.

Reflexive Verbs of Emotion

A number of verbs of emotion take **się**. Here are several of the more common of these verbs:

bać się *boję boisz*	be afraid
bawić się *-wię -wisz*	play
cieszyć się *-szę -szysz*	be glad
denerwować się *-wuję -wujesz*	be upset
dobrze się bawić	have a good time
dziwić się *-wię -wisz*	be surprised
martwić się *-wię -wisz*	worry
nudzić się *-dzę -dzisz*	be bored
przejmować się *-muję -mujesz*	be upset
wstydzić się *-dzę -dzisz*	be embarrassed

The following negated imperative forms of reflexive verbs of emotion are common.

nie bój się (nie BÓJ się)	don't be afraid
nie martw się (nie MARTW się)	don't worry
nie denerwuj się	don't be upset
nie przejmuj się	don't be concerned
nie wstydź się	don't be embarrassed

Reflexive-Only Verbs

Some verbs occur only with **się**, at least in a given meaning.

bać się *boję boisz*	be afraid, fear
dziać się *dzieje* (3sg.)	go on, happen
podobać się *-am -asz* (+ dat.)	be pleasing

starać się *-am -asz*   try
śmiać się *śmieję śmiejesz*   laugh
wydawać się *wydaje* (3sg.) (+ dat.)   seem
zdarzyć się *zdarzy* (3sg.) (pf.)   happen, occur

10. Important Sentence Constructions

Constructions Using the Infinitive

A number of common verbs take infinitive complements. One of the most useful of these verbs is **chcieć** *chcę chcesz want*, especially when used in the conditional mood in the sense "I'd like."

Chciał(a)bym zamówić rozmowę.	I'd like to place a call.

Other common verbs followed by the infinitive include **mieć** *mam masz be supposed to*, **musieć** *muszę musisz must, have to*, **starać się** *staram starasz try*, **umieć** *umiem umiesz know how*, and **woleć** *wolę wolisz prefer*. Three other useful words, **można** *one may*, **trzeba** *one ought*, and **wolno** *it is permitted*, are also followed by an infinitive and can be used to introduce a wide variety of impersonal statements and questions.

Można tu usiąść?	May one sit down here?
Trzeba to zrobić.	It's necessary to do that.
Tu nie wolno palić.	One may not smoke here.

Modal Expressions

The most important modal verbs refer to duty, need, and obligation. They are followed by an infinitive.

ought to, should	**powinien** *powinienem powinnam* 1pl. *powinniśmy*
need to, should	**musieć** *muszę musisz* OR **trzeba**
must, have to	**musieć** *muszę musisz* OR **mieć** *mam masz*
supposed to	**mieć** *mam masz*

Here is the conjugation of **powinien** fem. ***powinnam*** 1pl. masc.pers. ***powinniśmy*** in the present tense.

Singular

	Masc.	Fem.	Neut.
First-person	powinienem	powinnam	
Second-person	powinieneś	powinnaś	
Third-person	powinien	powinna	powinno

Plural

	Masc.Pers.	Other
First-person	powinniśmy	powinnyśmy
Second-person	powinniście	powinnyście
Third-person	powinni	powinny

Here are sentences using modal verbs:

Powinnaś się śpieszyć.	You (*fem.*) ought to hurry.
Muszę się uczyć.	I have to study.
Trzeba go zapytać.	One should ask him.
Mam być w domu o ósmej.	I'm supposed to be at home by eight.

Introducing Sentences

An identifying noun is introduced into conversation with the expression **to jest** *that/this is* or **to są** *those are*:

To jest mój kolega.	This is my colleague.
To jest dobra książka.	That's a good book.
To są moje okulary.	Those are my eyeglasses.

The expression **tu/tam jest** *here/there is* (pl. **tu/tam są**) is also often used:

Tu jest dobra nowa książka.	Here is a good new book.
Tam są nasi nowi sąsiedzi.	There are our new neighbors.

Identity Sentences

When two nouns are joined in an identity relationship, the verbal link is **to jest** (pl. **to są**). The verb **jest/są** may be omitted, but the **to** is obligatory.

Warszawa to (jest) stolica Polski.	Warsaw is the capital of Poland.
Ci państwo to (są) nasi nowi sąsiedzi.	Those people are our new neighbors.

This is different from the predicate noun construction discussed below, which does not use **to** but requires the instrumental case in the noun that follows. Often, the two constructions are virtually interchangeable.

Zosia to wspaniała sekretarka.   Zosia's an excellent secretary.

or

Zosia jest wspaniałą sekretarką.   Zosia's an excellent secretary.

Expressing *there is*

The verb **jest** (pl. **są**) is often used by itself to ask whether someone is "here/there" or whether an item is in stock.

Czy jest Marta?   Is Marta there?
Czy jest sok?   Is there any juice?
Czy są państwo Kowalczykowie? Are Mr. and Mrs. Kowalczyk here?
Czy są świeże pączki?   Are there any fresh doughnuts?

These questions are answered affirmatively by **jest** *there is*, **są** *there are*, or **nie ma** *there isn't / there aren't*. **Nie ma** takes the genitive case.

Nie ma Marty.   Marta is not (t)here.
Nie ma soku.   There is no juice.

The past of **nie ma** is **nie było**, and the future is **nie będzie**; both are neuter singular and both take the genitive case.

Nie było państwa Kowalczyków. Mr. and Mrs. Kowalczyk were not there.
Nie było świeżych pączków. There weren't any fresh doughnuts.

Predicate Nouns and Adjectives

A predicate noun or adjective is linked to the subject with a form of **być** *be*. A predicate noun is in the instrumental case.

Janek jest dobrym studentem.   Janek is a good student.
Ewa jest wymagającą   Ewa is a demanding teacher.
**   nauczycielką.**

In principle, the predicate noun construction, as opposed to the identity construction discussed above with **to jest/to są**, expresses inclusion in a set, as though one is saying that Janek belongs to the set of good students, or that Ewa belongs to the set of demanding teachers.

A predicate adjective is in the nominative case and agrees in gender with the subject.

Adam jest chory.	Adam is sick.
Marysia jest zdenerwowana.	Marysia is worried.

After the infinitive **być**, a predicate adjective may be in the instrumental case.

Chcę być kochaną.	I want to be loved.

Yes-No Questions

Questions to be answered by **tak** *yes* or **nie** *no* are expressed with the question word **czy** lit., *whether,* placed at the beginning of the sentence.

Czy pan jest gotowy?	Are you ready?
Czy to jest dobry film?	Is that a good movie?
Czy to nie jest Jan?	Isn't that Jan?

When a yes-no question centers on the verb, it is often answered with the verb, not with **tak** or **nie**.

—**Czy wypiłeś mleko?**	"Did you drink the milk?"
—**Wypiłem.**	"I drank it."

Negation

When a verb is negated, the negative particle **nie** is always placed immediately in front of it. Nothing can separate a verb from **nie**.

Nie mam czasu.	I don't have time.
Nie kupię tego.	I won't buy that.

When placed before one-syllable verbs, the particle **nie** takes the stress: NIE chcę, NIE wiem, NIE dam.

When using the equivalents of English *nothing, never, nowhere,* and so on, Polish also uses **nie** before the verb, thus creating a double or even triple or quadruple negative.

Nic nie mam.	I don't have anything.
Nikt tu nie mieszka.	No one lives here.
Nikt nic nikomu nie mówi.	No one says anything to anyone.

Another common word that occurs together with **nie** is **żaden, żadna, żadne** *none, not any.*

Żaden stół nie jest wolny.	No table is free.

Verbs that ordinarily take the accusative case take the genitive case when negated; compare the following sentences.

Oglądam telewizję.	I'm watching television.
Nie oglądam telewizji.	I'm not watching television.

The negation of *be* in its existential sense of *there is/are* is expressed by **nie ma** (past **nie było**, future **nie będzie**) plus the genitive case.

W sklepie jest piwo.	There is beer in the store.
Nie ma piwa w sklepie.	There is no beer in the store.
Nikogo interesującego tam nie było.	No one interesting was there.

Word Order

Word order in Polish tends to reflect the increasing informational importance of the elements in a sentence as one proceeds from left to right. Elements at the end typically carry logical stress and respond to implicit questions.

Jan (*nom.*) **kocha Marię** (*acc.*).	Jan loves Maria.

This sentence answers the question "Whom does Jan love?" ("Maria.") Compare this sentence with one in which the subject and object are reversed.

Marię kocha Jan.	Maria is loved by Jan. (*in effect*)

This sentence answers the question "Who loves Maria?" ("Jan.") Polish often makes use of the device of subject-object reversal to express the equivalent of passive voice.

Obudził mnie (*acc.*) **telefon** (*nom.*).	I was awakened by the telephone.

Background information is typically placed at the beginning of a sentence. Note the difference between Polish and English in this regard.

Jutro wieczorem w tej sali odbędzie się zebranie studentów.	There will be a meeting of students in this room tomorrow evening.

Manner adverbs tend to be placed earlier in a sentence rather than later. Here, too, note the difference between Polish and English.

On dobrze mówi po polsku.	He speaks Polish well.

Sentence Intonation

Sentence intonation is the slight rise or fall in pitch of the voice during speech. Polish sentences utilize three levels of intonation: mid, high, and low. Sentences can end on a rise or a fall, or be level at the end. High and low intonation is not radically different from mid intonation. Polish creates the impression of a moderately intoned language.

1. **Statement intonation.** A typical Polish declarative sentence opens at mid level, may rise slightly just before the end, but then drops to low level at the end.

On nie jest tak mi-ły, jak się wy-da-je.   He's not as nice as it appears.

2. **Yes-no questions.** Questions that expect an answer of either *yes* or *no* usually begin at mid level and end on a rise to high, possibly with a slight dip just before the rise.

Czy je-steś za-do-wo-lo-ny?   Are you satisfied?

Czy pa-ni mie-szka w War-sza-wie?   Do you live in Warsaw?

3. **WH questions.** Questions that ask *how, why, when, where, who, what, what kind,* and *which* typically begin at high level on the question word, and then fall to a low level for the remainder of the question.

Gdzie pa-ni mie-szka?   Where do you live?

Jak się pa-ni na-zy-wa?   What is your name?

For a more emphatic question, high level may be maintained until the end of the sentence, with a slight rise on the next to last syllable, then a dip to low.

Dla-cze-go pa-ni tak się śpie-szy?   Why are you in such a hurry?

It is important not to give WH questions the intonation of a yes-no question by ending on a high pitch. Aside from needing to learn this one rule, speakers of English are predisposed to have natural-sounding intonation in Polish.

4. **Manner adverbs.** Adverbs of manner do not usually occur at the end of a sentence, but rather before the verb, where they are emphasized intonationally.

On do-brze mó-wi po pol-sku.   He speaks Polish well.

11. The Most Important Polish Verbs

The 500-plus verbs in the list below are arranged alphabetically by the English gloss. The Polish verb is given in its infinitive form in boldface type, with finite forms in boldface italic. An abbreviated citation of the first- and second-person singular present tense is given, and of the third-person plural if it is irregular. Irregular or difficult imperatives are given in the second-person singular. Irregular or difficult past tense forms are given in the third-person masculine singular, third-person feminine singular, and third-person masculine personal plural forms. Other forms are easily derived from these forms (see Chapter 9). For very irregular verbs, all forms may be given.

Verbs are assumed to belong to the imperfective (impf.) aspect and to be transitive unless otherwise noted. Perfective (pf.) verbs are given following their imperfective partner. Derived imperfective verbs in -*ać* are of the -*am -asz* type unless otherwise noted. For more complete syntactic information, consult a dictionary.

The following abbreviations are used in this chapter:

3sg.	third-person singular	indet.	indeterminate
acc.	accusative case	inf.	infinitive
dat.	dative case	instr.	instrumental case
det.	determinate	intr.	intransitive
e.g.	for example	loc.	locative case
fut.	future tense	pf.	perfective aspect
gen.	genitive case	refl.	reflexive
imp.	imperative mood	tr.	transitive
impf.	imperfective aspect		

accept (1)	**akceptować** *-tuję -tujesz*; pf. **zaakceptować**
accept (2)	**przyjmować** *-muję -mujesz*; pf. **przyjąć** *-jmę -jmiesz* imp. *przyjmij* (*receive*)
add	**dodawać** *-daję -dajesz* imp. *dodawaj*; pf. **dodać** *-dam -dasz -dadzą* imp. *dodaj*
admire	**podziwiać** *-am -asz*
admit (1)	**przyznawać się** *-naję -najesz* imp. *przyznawaj*; pf. **przyznać się** *-am -asz*; **do** (+ gen.) (*confess to*)
admit (2)	**wpuszczać** *-am -asz*; pf. **wpuścić** *-szczę -ścisz* (*let in*)
advise	**radzić** *-dzę -dzisz*; pf. **poradzić**; (+ dat.)
affect	**wpływać** *-am -asz*; pf. **wpłynąć** *-nę -niesz*; **na** (+ acc.) (*have an effect on*)
agree	**zgadzać się** *-am -asz*; pf. **zgodzić się** *-dzę -dzisz*; **z** (+ instr.) *with*
aid	**sprzyjać** *-am -asz*; (+ dat.) *with* (*favor*)
ail	**dolegać** *-am -asz*; (+ dat.)
aim	**celować** *-luję -lujesz*; pf. **wycelować**; **do** (+ gen.) *at*
allow	**pozwalać** *-am -asz*; pf. **pozwolić** *-lę -lisz* imp. *pozwól*; (+ dat.)
answer	**odpowiadać** *-am -asz*; pf. **odpowiedzieć** *-powiem -powiesz -powiedzą* imp. *odpowiedz*; **na** (+ acc.)
apologize	**przepraszać** *-am -asz*; pf. **przeprosić** *-szę -sisz*; **za** (+ acc.) *for*
appear (1)	**pojawiać się** *-am -asz*; pf. **pojawić się** *-wię -wisz* (*come into view*)
appear (2)	**wydawać się** *-daję -dajesz*; pf. **wydać się** *-da -dadzą*; usually 3rd-person (+ dat.) (*seem*)
apply (1)	**stosować** *-suję -sujesz*; pf. **zastosować** (*use*)
apply (2)	**zgłaszać się** *-am -asz*; pf. **zgłosić się** *-szę -sisz*; **do** (+ gen.) *to* (e.g., *apply for work*)
appreciate	**doceniać** *-am -asz*; pf. **docenić** *-nię -nisz*
approve (1)	**zatwierdzać** *-am -asz*; pf. **zatwierdzić** *-dzę -dzisz* (*confirm*)
approve (2)	**pochwalać** *-am -asz*; pf. **pochwalić** *-lę -lisz* (*consider good*)
argue	**kłócić się** *-cę -cisz*; pf. **pokłócić się**; **z** (+ instr.) *with*

arrange (1)	**urządzać** *-am -asz*; pf. **urządzić** *-dzę -dzisz* (*an apartment or a party*)
arrange (2)	**organizować** *-zuję -zujesz*; pf. **zorganizować** (*organize*)
arrange (3)	**układać** *-am -asz*; pf. **ułożyć** *-żę -żysz* imp. *ułóż* (*put in order*)
ask (1)	**prosić** *-szę -sisz*; pf. **poprosić**; **o** (+ acc.) *(ask) for*
ask (2)	**pytać** *-am -asz*; pf. **zapytać** OR **spytać**; **o** (+ acc.) *(ask) about*
attack	**atakować** *-kuję -kujesz*; pf. **zaatakować**
bake	**piec** *piekę pieczesz* past *piekł piekła piekli*; pf. **upiec**
bathe	**kąpać** *-pię -piesz*; pf. **wykąpać**
be	**być** *jestem jesteś jest jesteśmy jesteście są* fut. *będę będziesz będzie będziemy będziecie będą* imp. *bądź*
be able	**móc** *mogę możesz* past *mógł mogła mogli*; + inf.
be afraid of	**bać się** *boję boisz* imp. *bój się*; (+ gen.)
be ashamed	**wstydzić się** *-dzę -dzisz*; pf. **zewstydzić się**; (+ gen.) *of*
be born	**rodzić się** *-dzę -dzisz*; pf. **urodzić się**
be glad	**cieszyć się** *-szę -szysz*; pf. **ucieszyć się**; **z** (+ gen.) *of*
be late	**spóźniać się** *-am -asz*; pf. **spóźnić się** *-nię -nisz*; **na** (+ acc.) *for*
be sick	**chorować** *-ruję -rujesz*; pf. **zachorować** (*fall sick*) OR **pochorować** (*be sick for a while*)
be sorry	**żałować** *-łuję -łujesz*; pf. **pożałować**; (+ gen.) *for*
be surprised	**dziwić się** *-wię -wisz*; pf. **zdziwić się**; (+ dat.) *at*
be wrong	**mylić się** *-lę -lisz*; pf. **pomylić się**
bear	**znosić** *znoszę znosisz*; pf. **znieść** *zniosę zniesiesz* past *zniósł zniosła znieśli* imp. *znieś* (*endure*). *See also* carry.
beat (1)	**bić** *biję bijesz*; pf. **pobić** (*strike*)
beat (2)	**pokonywać** *-nuję -nujesz*; pf. **pokonać** *-am -asz* (*conquer*)
become (1)	**zostawać** *-staję -stajesz*; pf. **zostać** *-stanę -staniesz* imp. *zostań* (*get to be*)
become (2)	**stawać się** *staję stajesz*; pf. **stać się** *stanę staniesz*
begin	**zaczynać** *-am -asz*; pf. **zacząć** *-cznę -czniesz* imp. *zacznij*; intr. — **się**

behave	**zachowywać się** *-wuję -wujesz*; pf. **zachować się** *-am -asz*
believe	**wierzyć** *-rzę -rzysz*; pf. **uwierzyć**; (+ dat.) (*believe someone*); **w** (+ acc.) *in*
belong	**należeć** *-żę -żysz*; **do** (+ gen.) *to*
bet	**zakładać się** *-am -asz*; pf. **założyć się** *-żę -żysz* imp. *załóż się*; **o** (+ acc.) *on*
bite	**gryźć** *gryzę gryziesz* past *gryzł gryzła gryźli* imp. *gryź*; pf. **ugryźć** OR **pogryźć**
blame	**obwiniać** *-am -asz*; pf. **obwinić** *-nię -nisz*
blossom	**kwitnąć** *-nę -niesz* past *kwitł kwitła kwitli*; pf. **zakwitnąć**
blow (1)	**dmuchać** *-am -asz*; pf. **dmuchnąć** *-nę -niesz* (*puff*)
blow (2)	**wiać** *wieję wiejesz*; pf. **zawiać**; usually 3rd-person (*of the wind*)
boil	**gotować** *-tuję -tujesz*; pf. **zagotować**; intr. — **się**
bother (1)	**przeszkadzać** *-am -asz*; pf. **przeszkodzić** *-dzę -dzisz*; (+ dat.) (*interfere with*)
bother (2)	**irytować** *-tuję -tujesz*; pf. **zirytować** (*annoy*)
break (1)	**łamać** *-mię -miesz*; pf. **złamać** OR **połamać**; intr. — **się**
break (2)	**pękać** *-am -asz*; pf. **pęknąć** *-nę -niesz* (*burst, shatter*)
break (3)	**przerywać** *-am -asz*; pf. **przerwać** *-rwę -rwiesz* imp. *przerwij* (*interrupt*)
breathe	**oddychać** *-am -asz*; pf. **odetchnąć** *-nę -niesz*
bring (1)	**przynosić** *-noszę -nosisz*; pf. **przynieść** *-niosę -niesiesz* past *przyniósł przyniosła przynieśli* imp. *przynieś*
bring (2)	**przywozić** *-żę -zisz*; pf. **przywieźć** *-wiozę -wieziesz* past *przywiózł przywiozła przywieźli* imp. *przywieź* (*bring by vehicle*)
build	**budować** *-duję -dujesz*; pf. **wybudować** OR **zbudować** OR **pobudować**
burn	**palić** *-lę -lisz*; pf. **spalić**; intr. — **się**
bury	**zakopywać** *-puję -pujesz*; pf. **zakopać** *-pię -piesz*
buy	**kupować** *-puję -pujesz*; pf. **kupić** *-pię -pisz*
call (1)	**wołać** *-am -asz*; pf. **zawołać** (*shout*); **do** (+ gen.) *to*
call (2)	**dzwonić** *-nię -nisz*; pf. **zadzwonić** (*telephone*); **do** (+ gen.)
call (3)	*See* name.

call off	**odwoływać** *-łuję -łujesz*; pf. **odwołać** *-am -asz*
carry (1)	**nosić** *noszę nosisz* (indet.); det. **nieść** *niosę niesiesz* past *niósł niosła nieśli* imp. *nieś*; pf. **ponieść** OR **zanieść** (*carry by hand, wear*)
carry (2)	**wozić** *wożę wozisz* (indet.); det. **wieźć** *wiozę wieziesz* past *wiózł wiozła wieźli* imp. *wieź*; pf. **powieźć** OR **zawieźć** (*carry by vehicle*)
catch	**łapać** *-pię -piesz*; pf. **złapać**
cause (1)	**powodować** *-duję -dujesz*; pf. **spowodować** (*bring about*)
cause (2)	**sprawiać** *-am -asz*; pf. **sprawić** *-wię -wisz* (*create*)
change (1)	**zmieniać** *-am -asz*; pf. **zmienić** *-nię -nisz*
change (2)	**zamieniać** *-am -asz*; pf. **zamienić** *-nię -nisz* (*replace*)
change (3)	**przebierać** *-am -asz*; pf. **przebrać** *-biorę -bierzesz*; refl. — **się** (*change clothes*)
change (4)	**przemieniać się** *-am -asz*; pf. **przemienić się** *-nię -nisz*; **w** (+ acc.) *change into*
check	**sprawdzać** *-am -asz*; pf. **sprawdzić** *-dzę -dzisz*
chew	**żuć** *żuję żujesz*
choose	**wybierać** *-am -asz*; pf. **wybrać** *-biorę -bierzesz*
clean	**czyścić** *czyszczę czyścisz*; pf. **wyczyścić** OR **poczyścić**
clean up	**sprzątać** *-am -asz*; pf. **posprzątać** OR **sprzątnąć** *-nę -niesz* (*tidy*)
close	**zamykać** *-am -asz*; pf. **zamknąć** *-nę -niesz*; intr. — **się**
comb	**czesać** *czeszę czeszesz*; pf. **uczesać**; refl. — **się** (*one's hair*)
come (1)	**przychodzić** *-dzę -dzisz*; pf. **przyjść** *-jdę -jdziesz* past *przyszedł przyszła przyszli* imp. *przyjdź* (*come on foot*)
come (2)	**przyjeżdżać** *-am -asz*; pf. **przyjechać** *-jadę -jedziesz* imp. *przyjedź* (*come by vehicle*)
complain	**narzekać** *-am -asz*; **na** (+ acc.) *about*
concern (1)	**dotyczyć** *-czy*; usually 3rd-person (+ gen.) (*apply to*)
concern (2)	**obchodzić** *-dzi*; usually 3rd-person (*be of concern to*)
consider (1)	**uważać** *-am -asz* (*think*)
consider (2)	**zastanawiać się** *-am -asz*; pf. **zastanowić się** *-wię -wisz* imp. *zastanów*; **nad** (+ instr.) (*give thought to*)
consist of	**składać się** *-am -asz*; **z** (+ gen.)
contain	**zawierać** *-am -asz;* pf. **zawrzeć** *-rę -rzesz*

cook	**gotować** *-tuję -tujesz*; pf. **ugotować**
cost	**kosztować** *-tuję -tujesz*
cough	**kaszlać** *-lę -lesz* imp. *kaszl*; pf. **kaszlnąć** *-nę -niesz*
count	**liczyć** *-czę -czysz*; pf. **policzyć**; intr. — **się**
cover	**pokrywać** *-am -asz*; pf. **pokryć** *-kryję -kryjesz*
crawl (1)	**czołgać się** *-am -asz*
crawl (2)	**raczkować** *-kuję -kujesz* (*of a baby*)
create	**tworzyć** *-rzę -rzysz*; pf. **stworzyć** OR **utworzyć**
cry	**płakać** *płaczę płaczesz*; pf. **zapłakać**
cure	**leczyć** *-czę -czysz*; pf. **wyleczyć**
cut (1)	**ciąć** *tnę tniesz* imp. *tnij*; pf. **pociąć** (*nick*)
cut (2)	**kroić** *kroję kroisz* imp. *krój*; pf. **pokroić** (*slice*)
cut (3)	**ostrzygać** *-am -asz*; pf. **ostrzyc** *-ygę -yżesz* past *ostrzygł ostrzygła ostrzygli*; refl. — **się** (*cut hair*)
dance	**tańczyć** *-czę -czysz*; pf. **potańczyć** OR **zatańczyć**
dare (1)	**śmieć** *-em -esz* imp. *śmiej* (*be bold*)
dare (2)	**wyzywać** *-am -asz*; pf. **wyzwać** *-zwę -źwiesz* imp. *wezwij* (*challenge*)
decide (1)	**decydować** *-duję -dujesz*; pf. **zdecydować** (*determine*)
decide (2)	**postanawiać** *-am -asz*; pf. **postanowić** *-wię -wisz* imp. *postanów*
defend	**bronić** *-nię -nisz*; pf. **zabronić**; (+ gen.)
demand (1)	**wymagać** *-am -asz*; (+ gen.) (*require*)
demand (2)	**domagać się** *-am -asz*; (+ gen.) (*insist on*)
depend	**zależeć** *-żę -żysz*; **od** (+ gen.) *on*
desire (1)	**życzyć** *-czę -czysz*; pf. **zażyczyć**; (+ gen.)
desire (2)	**pragnąć** *-nę -niesz*; pf. **zapragnąć**; (+ gen.) (*want*)
desire (3)	**pożądać** *-am -asz* (*covet, want to possess*)
despise	**gardzić** *-dzę -dzisz*; pf. **wzgardzić**; (+ instr.) (*look down on*)
destroy	**niszczyć** *-czę -czysz*; pf. **zniszczyć**
develop	**rozwijać** *-am -asz*; pf. **rozwinąć** *-nę -niesz*; intr. — **się**
die (1)	**umierać** *-am -asz*; pf. **umrzeć** *umrę umrzesz* past *umarł umarła umarli* imp. *umrzyj*

die (2)	**zemrzeć -mrę -mrzesz** (pf. only) (*expire*)
die (3)	**zamierać -am -asz**; pf. **zamrzeć -mrę -mrzesz** (*die down*)
die (4)	**zdychać -am -asz**; pf. **zdechnąć -nę -niesz** past *zdechł zdechła* (*of an animal*)
dig	**kopać -pię -piesz**; pf. **zakopać**
divide	**dzielić -lę -lisz**; pf. **podzielić**
do	**robić -bię -bisz** imp. *rób*; pf. **zrobić**
doubt	**wątpić -pię -pisz** imp. *wątp*; pf. **zwątpić** OR **powątpić**; **w** (+ acc.)
draw	**rysować -suję -sujesz**; pf. **narysować** (*sketch*)
dream (1)	**marzyć -rzę -rzysz**; pf. **wymarzyć** (*daydream*)
dream (2)	**śnić się** *śnię śnisz*; pf. **przyśnić się**; usually 3rd-person (+ dat.)
dress	**ubierać -am -asz**; pf. **ubrać** *ubiorę ubierzesz*; refl. — **się**
drink	**pić** *piję pijesz*; pf. **wypić**
drive	**prowadzić -dzę -dzisz**; pf. **poprowadzić** (*operate a vehicle*)
drip	**kapać -pię -piesz**; pf. **kapnąć -nę -niesz**
drop	**upuszczać -am -asz**; pf. **upuścić -szczę -ścisz** (*let fall*)
drown (1)	**tonąć -nę -niesz**; pf. **utonąć**; intr.
drown (2)	**topić -pię -pisz**; pf. **utopić**; tr.; — **się** (*drown oneself on purpose*)
dry	**suszyć -szę -szysz**; pf. **wysuszyć** OR **ususzyć**
earn	**zarabiać -am -asz**; pf. **zarobić -bię -bisz**
eat	**jeść** *jem jesz jedzą* past *jadł jadła jedli* imp. *jedz*; pf. **zjeść**
encourage	**zachęcać -am -asz**; pf. **zachęcić -cę -cisz**
endure (1)	**znosić** *znoszę znosisz*; pf. **znieść** *zniosę zniesiesz* past *zniósł zniosła znieśli* imp. *znieś* (*stand*)
endure (2)	**trwać -am -asz**; pf. **przetrwać** (*last*)
enter (1)	**wchodzić -dzę -dzisz** imp. *wchodź*; pf. **wejść** *wejdę wejdziesz* past *wszedł weszła weszli* imp. *wejdź*; **do** (+ gen.) (*enter on foot*)
enter (2)	**wjeżdżać -am -asz**; pf. **wjechać** *wjadę wjedziesz* imp. *wjedź*; **do** (+ gen.) (*enter by vehicle*)

escape	**uciekać** *-am -asz*; pf. **uciec** *ucieknę uciekniesz* past *uciekł uciekła uciekli*
exchange	**wymieniać** *-am -asz*; pf. **wymienić** *-nię -nisz*
exist	**istnieć** *-nieję -niejesz*; pf. **zaistnieć**
expect (1)	**spodziewać się** *-am -asz*; (+ gen.) (*await*)
expect (2)	**przypuszczać** *-am -asz*; pf. **przypuścić** *-szczę -ścisz* (*suppose*)
experience	**doświadczać** *-am -asz*; pf. **doświadczyć** *-czę -czysz*; (+ gen.)
explain	**tłumaczyć** *-czę -czysz*; pf. **wytłumaczyć**
express	**wyrażać** *-am -asz*; pf. **wyrazić** *-żę -zisz*
faint	**mdleć** *-leję -lejesz*; pf. **zemdleć**
fall	**padać** *-am -asz*; pf. **paść** *padnę padniesz* past *padł padła padli* imp. *padnij*
fall asleep	**zasypiać** *-am -asz*; pf. **zasnąć** *zasnę zaśniesz* imp. *zaśnij*
fall in love	**zakochiwać się** *-chuję -chujesz*; pf. **zakochać się**; **w** (+ loc.) *with*
fear	**obawiać się** *-am -asz*; (+ gen.)
feed	**karmić** *-mię -misz*; pf. **nakarmić**
feel (1)	**czuć** *-uję -ujesz*; pf. **poczuć** (*sense*)
feel (2)	**czuć się** *-uję -ujesz*; pf. **poczuć się** (*feel good, bad, etc.*)
feel (3)	**dotykać** *-am -asz*; pf. **dotknąć** *-nę -niesz* imp. *dotknij* (*touch*)
fight (1)	**bić się** *biję bijesz*; pf. **pobić się**
fight (2)	**walczyć** *-czę -czysz*; **o** (+ acc.) *for*
fill	**napełniać** *-am -asz*; pf. **napełnić** *-nię -nisz* imp. *napełń*
find (1)	**znajdować** *-duję -dujesz*; pf. **znaleźć** *znajdę znajdziesz* past *znalazł znalazła znaleźli* imp. *znajdź* (*locate*)
find (2)	**zastawać** *-staję -stajesz*; pf. **zastać** *-stanę -staniesz* imp. *zastań* (*come upon*)
find out	**dowiadywać się** *-duję -dujesz*; pf. **dowiedzieć się** *-wiem -wiesz -wiedzą*; (+ gen.)
finish	**kończyć** *-czę -czysz*; pf. **skończyć**
fit	**pasować** *-suję -sujesz*; pf. **dopasować** *-suję -sujesz*; **do** (+ gen.)

fix	**naprawiać** *-am -asz*; pf. **naprawić** *-wię -wisz* (*repair*)
flow	**ciec** *ciekę ciekniesz* past *ciekł ciekła ciekli*
fly	**latać** *-am -asz* (indet.); det. **lecieć** *-cę -cisz*; pf. **polecieć**
fold	**składać** *-am -asz*; pf. **złożyć** *-żę -żysz* (*put together*)
follow	**następować** *-puję -pujesz*; pf. **nastąpić** *-pię -pisz* (*come after*)
forget	**zapominać** *-am -asz*; pf. **zapomnieć** *-nę -nisz* imp. *zapomnij*; (+ gen.)
freeze (1)	**marznąć** *-znę -zniesz* past *marzł marzła marźli*; pf. **zmarznąć**; intr.
freeze (2)	**zamrażać** *-am -asz*; pf. **zamrozić** *-żę -zisz*; tr.
frown (1)	**marszczyć brwi** *-czę -czysz*; pf. **zmarszczyć brwi**
frown (2)	**zachmurzać się** *-am -asz*; pf. **zachmurzyć się** *-rzę -rzysz* (*become gloomy*)
gather	**zbierać** *-am -asz*; pf. **zebrać** *zbiorę zbierzesz*; intr. — **się** (*meet*)
get (1)	**dostawać** *-staję -stajesz*; pf. **dostać** *-stanę -staniesz* imp. *dostań* (*receive*)
get (2)	**zostawać** *-staję -stajesz*; pf. **zostać** *-stanę -staniesz* imp. *zostań* (*become*)
get (3)	**robić się** *-bię -bisz*; pf. **zrobić się** (*become*)
get in/on	**wsiadać** *-am -asz*; pf. **wsiąść** *wsiądę wsiądziesz* past *wsiadł wsiadła wsiedli*; **do** (+ gen.) (*a car, bus, etc.*)
get in(to)	**dostawać się** *-staję -stajesz*; pf. **dostać się** *-stanę -staniesz* imp. *dostań*; **do** (+ gen.) (*a town, place*)
get off/out	**wysiadać** *-am -asz*; pf. **wysiąść** *wysiądę wysiądziesz* past *wysiadł wysiadła wysiedli*; **z** (+ gen.) *of* (*a car, bus, etc.*)
get up	**wstawać** *wstaję wstajesz*; pf. **wstać** *wstanę wstaniesz* imp. *wstań* (*arise*)
give	**dawać** *daję dajesz*; pf. **dać** *dam dasz dadzą* imp. *daj*; (+ acc.)
give up	**poddawać się** *-daję -dajesz*; pf. **poddać się** *-dam -dasz -dadzą* (*yield*)
glance	**spoglądać** *-am -asz*; pf. **spojrzeć** *-rzę -rzysz* imp. *spójrz*; **na** (+ acc.) *at*

go (1)	**chodzić** *-dzę -dzisz* imp. *chodź* (indet.); det. **iść idę idziesz** past *szedł szła szli* imp. *idź*; pf. **pójść pójdę pójdziesz** past *poszedł poszła poszli* imp. *pójdź* (*go on foot*)
go (2)	**jeździć** *-żdżę -ździsz* imp. *jeźdź* (indet.); det. **jechać jadę jedziesz** imp. *jedź*; pf. **pojechać** (*go by vehicle*)
grab	**chwytać** *-am -asz*; pf. **chwycić** *-cę -cisz*; **za** (+ acc.) *by*
grant	**przyznawać** *-naję -najesz* imp. *przyznawaj*; pf. **przyznać** *-am -asz*
greet	**witać** *-am -asz*; pf. **powitać** OR **przywitać**
grow (1)	**rosnąć** *-snę -śniesz* past *rósł rosła rośli*; pf. **urosnąć**
grow (2)	**uprawiać** *-am -asz* (*cultivate*)
hang (1)	**wisieć** *-szę -sisz* (*dangle*)
hang (2)	**wieszać** *-am -asz*; pf. **powiesić** *-szę -sisz*; tr.; refl. — **się**
happen (1)	**dziać się** *dzieje*; pf. **stać się** *stanie*; usually 3sg. (*go on*)
happen (2)	**zdarzać się** *-a*; pf. **zdarzyć się** *zdarzy*; usually 3sg. (*occur*)
harm	**szkodzić** *-dzę -dzisz*; pf. **zaszkodzić** (+ dat.)
hate	**nienawidzić** *-dzę -dzisz*; pf. **znienawidzić** *-dzę -dzisz* (+ gen.)
have	**mieć** *mam masz ma mamy macie mają* imp. *miej*
hear	**słyszeć** *-szę -szysz*; pf. **usłyszeć**
help	**pomagać** *-am -asz*; pf. **pomóc** *-mogę -możesz* past *pomógł pomogła pomogli* imp. *pomóż* (+ dat.)
hesitate	**wahać się** *-am -asz*; pf. **zawahać się**
hire	**angażować** *-żuję -żujesz*; pf. **zaangażować**
hit (1)	**uderzać** *-am -asz*; pf. **uderzyć** *-rzę -rzysz* (*strike*)
hit (2)	**trafiać** *-am -asz*; pf. **trafić** *-fię -fisz* (*a target*)
hold	**trzymać** *-am -asz*; pf. **potrzymać**
hope	**mieć nadzieję.** *See* have.
hug	**obejmować** *-muję -mujesz*; pf. **objąć** *obejmę obejmiesz* imp. *obejmij*
hunt	**polować** *-luję -lujesz*; pf. **upolować** *-luję -lujesz*; **na** (+ acc.) *for*
hurry	**śpieszyć się** *-szę -szysz*; pf. **pośpieszyć się** (*be in a hurry*)
hurt	**boleć** *boli*; only 3rd-person (+ acc.)

imagine	**wyobrażać sobie** *-am -asz*; pf. **wyobrazić sobie** *-żę -zisz*
indicate	**wskazywać** *-zuję -zujesz*; pf. **wskazać** *-żę -żesz*; **na** (+ acc.)
interest	**interesować** *-suję -sujesz*; pf. **zainteresować**; — **się** (+ instr.) (*be interested in*)
introduce (1)	**wprowadzać** *-am -asz*; pf. **wprowadzić** *-dzę -dzisz*; **do** (+ gen.)
introduce (2)	**przedstawiać** *-am -asz*; pf. **przedstawić** *-wię -wisz*; (+ dat.) (*present*)
invent	**wynajdować** *-duję -dujesz*; pf. **wynaleźć** *-najdę -najdziesz* past **wynalazł wynalazła wynaleźli**
invite	**zapraszać** *-am -asz*; pf. **zaprosić** *-szę -sisz*
join (1)	**łączyć** *-czę -czysz*; pf. **złączyć** OR **połączyć**; **z** (+ instr.) *to* (*combine, connect*)
join (2)	**wstępować** *-puję -pujesz*; pf. **wstąpić** *-pię -pisz*; **do** (+ gen.) (*enroll, enlist in*)
joke	**żartować** *-tuję -tujesz*; pf. **zażartować**
judge	**osądzać** *-am -asz*; pf. **osądzić** (*evaluate*)
jump	**skakać skaczę skaczesz**; pf. **skoczyć skoczę skoczysz**
keep (1)	**zachowywać** *-wuję -wujesz*; pf. **zachować** *-am -asz* (*retain*)
keep (2)	**utrzymywać** *-muję -mujesz*; pf. **utrzymać** *-am -asz* (*maintain*)
kick	**kopać** *-pię -piesz*; pf. **kopnąć** *-nę -niesz* imp. **kopnij**
kill	**zabijać** *-am -asz*; pf. **zabić** *-iję -ijesz*
kiss	**całować** *-łuję -łujesz*; pf. **pocałować** OR **ucałować**; **w** (+ acc.)
knock	**pukać** *-am -asz*; pf. **zapukać**; **do** (+ gen.) *on*
know (1)	**wiedzieć wiem wiesz wiedzą** (*know information*)
know (2)	**znać** *-am -asz* (*know someone or something*)
know how	**umieć** *-iem -iesz*; + inf.
land	**lądować** *-duję -dujesz*; pf. **wylądowywać** (*of an airplane*)
last	**trwać** *-am -asz*; pf. **potrwać**; usually 3rd-person
laugh	**śmiać się** *-ieję -iejesz*; pf. **zaśmiać się**; **z** (+ gen.) *at*
lay	*See* put.

lead (1)	**prowadzić** *-dzę -dzisz*; pf. **poprowadzić**
lead (2)	**kierować** *-ruję -rujesz*; pf. **pokierować**; (+ instr.) (e.g., *direct an orchestra*)
lead (3)	**przodować** *-duję -dujesz* (*be the best*)
lean (1)	**opierać** *-am -asz*; pf. **oprzeć** *oprę oprzesz* past *oparł oparła oparli*; intr. — **się** (*support*)
lean (2)	**pochylać** *-am -asz*; pf. **pochylić** *-lę -lisz* (*incline*); intr. — **się**
learn	**uczyć się** *uczę uczysz* (*study*); pf. **nauczyć się** (*learn*); (+ gen.)
leave (1)	**wychodzić** *-dzę -dzisz*; pf. **wyjść** *-jdę -jdziesz* past *wyszedł wyszła wyszli* imp. *wyjdź* (*leave on foot*)
leave (2)	**wyjeżdżać** *-am -asz*; pf. **wyjechać** *-jadę -jedziesz* imp. *wyjedź* (*leave by vehicle*)
leave (3)	**zostawiać** *-am -asz*; pf. **zostawić** *-wię -wisz* (*leave behind*)
leave (4)	**opuszczać** *-am -asz*; pf. **opuścić** *-szczę -ścisz* (*abandon*)
lick	**lizać** *-żę -żesz*; pf. **polizać**
lie (1)	**kłamać** *-mię -miesz*; pf. **skłamać** (*tell a lie*)
lie (2)	**leżeć** *-żę -żysz*; pf. **poleżeć** (*recline*)
lie down	**kłaść się** *kładę kładziesz* imp. *kładź*; pf. **położyć się** *-żę -żysz* imp. *połóż*
lift	**podnosić** *-noszę -nosisz*; pf. **podnieść** *-niosę -niesiesz* past *podniósł podniosła podnieśli* imp. *podnieś*
like	**lubić** *-bię -bisz*; pf. **polubić**
listen (to)	**słuchać** *-am -asz*; pf. **posłuchać**; (+ gen.)
live (1)	**żyć** *żyję żyjesz*; pf. **przeżyć** (*be alive*)
live (2)	**mieszkać** *-am -asz* (*reside*)
loan	**pożyczać** *-am -asz*; pf. **pożyczyć** *-czę -czysz*
lock	**zamykać** *-am -asz*; pf. **zamknąć** *-nę -niesz*; intr. — **się**
look (1)	**patrzeć** *-trzę -trzysz*; pf. **popatrzeć**; **na** (+ acc.) *at*
look (2)	**wyglądać** *-am -asz* (*appear*)
look after	**pilnować** *-nuję -nujesz*; pf. **dopilnować** OR **przypilnować** OR **popilnować**; (+ gen.)
look for	**szukać** *-am -asz*; (+ gen.)

lose (1)	**gubić** *-bię -bisz*; pf. **zgubić** (*misplace*)
lose (2)	**przegrywać** *-am -asz*; pf. **przegrać** *-am -asz* (*lose a game*)
love	**kochać** *-am -asz*. *See also* fall in love, make love.
make (1)	**robić** *-bię -bisz* imp. *rób*; pf. **zrobić** (*do*)
make (2)	**zarabiać** *-am -asz*; pf. **zarobić** *-bię -bisz* (*earn*)
make (3)	**zmuszać** *-am -asz*; pf. **zmusić** *-szę -sisz* (*force*)
make love	**kochać się** *-am -asz*; pf. **pokochać się**; **z** (+ instr.) *with*
manage (1)	**zarządzać** *-am -asz*; pf. **zarządzić** *-dzę -dzisz*; (+ instr.) (*administer*)
manage (2)	**zdołać** *-am -asz* (pf.); + inf. (*manage to do*)
manage (3)	**zdążyć** *-żę -żysz* (pf.); + inf. (*manage to do on time*)
manage (4)	**potrafić** *-fię -fisz* (impf. or pf.); + inf. (*be able*)
marry (1)	**pobierać się** *-am -asz*; pf. **pobrać się** *-biorę -bierzesz*
marry (2)	**żenić się** *-nię -nisz*; pf. **ożenić się**; **z** (+ instr.) (*of a man only*)
marry (3)	**wychodzić za mąż** *-dzę -dzisz*; pf. **wyjść za mąż** *-jdę -jdziesz* past *wyszła*; (*of a woman only*)
mean (1)	**znaczyć** *-czę -czysz*; usually 3rd-person (*signify*)
mean (2)	**chcieć powiedzieć** (*want to say*). *See* want.
meet (1)	**spotykać** *-am -asz*; pf. **spotkać**; reciprocal — **się**; **z** (+ instr.) (*encounter*)
meet (2)	**poznawać** *-znaję -znajesz*; pf. **poznać** *-am -asz* (*become acquainted*)
melt	**topić** *-pię -pisz*; pf. **utopić**; intr. — **się**
mind	**pilnować** *-nuję -nujesz*; pf. **przypilnować** OR **popilnować**; (+ gen.) (*look after*)
miss (1)	**chybiać** *-am -asz*; pf. **chybić** *-bię -bisz* (*a target*)
miss (2)	**tęsknić** *-nię -nisz*; pf. **zatęsknić**; **za** (+ instr.) (*long for*)
mix	**mieszać** *-am -asz*; pf. **zmieszać** OR **wymieszać** OR **zamieszać**
mix up	**mylić** *-lę -lisz*; pf. **pomylić** (*mistake*)
move (1)	**ruszać** *-am -asz*; pf. **ruszyć** *-szę -szysz* (*touch*)
move (2)	**przeprowadzać się** *-am -asz*; pf. **przeprowadzić się** *-dzę -dzisz* (*change abode*)

must	**musieć** *-szę -sisz*; + inf.
name	**nazywać** *-am -asz*; pf. **nazwać** *-zwę -zwiesz*; imp. *nazwij*; intr. — **się** (*be called*)
need	**potrzebować** *-buję -bujesz*; (+ gen.)
notice	**zauważać** *-am -asz*; pf. **zauważyć** *-żę -żysz*
obey	**słuchać** *-am -asz*; pf. **posłuchać**; (+ gen.)
occupy	**zajmować** *-muję -mujesz*; pf. **zająć** *-jmę -jmiesz* imp. *zajmij*; — **się** (+ instr.) (*occupy oneself*)
offend	**obrażać** *-am -asz*; pf. **obrazić** *-żę -zisz*
open	**otwierać** *-am -asz*; pf. **otworzyć** *-rzę -rzysz* imp. *otwórz*; intr. — **się**
order (1)	**rozkazywać** *-zuję -zujesz*; pf. **rozkazać** *-żę -żesz* (*command*)
order (2)	**zamawiać** *-am -asz*; pf. **zamówić** *-wię -wisz* (*place an order*)
pack	**pakować** *-kuję -kujesz*; pf. **spakować** OR **zapakować**
paint	**malować** *-luję -lujesz*; pf. **pomalować** OR **namalować**
pass (1)	**przechodzić** *-dzę -dzisz*; pf. **przejść** *-jdę -jdziesz* past *przeszedł przeszła przeszli* imp. *przejdź* (*go through/past*)
pass (2)	**zdać** *zdam zdasz zdadzą* (pf.) (*pass an examination*)
pass (3)	**pasować** *-suję -sujesz*; pf. **spasować** (*in cards*)
pay	**płacić** *-cę -cisz*; pf. **zapłacić**; **za** (+ acc.) *for*
phone	**dzwonić** *-nię -nisz*; pf. **zadzwonić**; **do** (+ gen.)
pick (1)	**wybierać** *-am -asz*; pf. **wybrać** *-biorę bierzesz* (*choose*)
pick (2)	**zrywać** *-am -asz*; pf. **zerwać** *-rwę -rwiesz* imp. *zerwij* (e.g., *fruit*)
pity	**litować się** *-tuję -tujesz;* pf. **ulitować się**; **nad** (+ instr.)
place	**stawiać** *-am -asz*; pf. **postawić** *-wię -wisz* (*put in a standing position*)
plant	**wsadzać** *-am -asz*; pf. **wsadzić** *-dzę -dzisz*
play (1)	**grać** *-am -asz*; pf. **pograć** OR **zagrać**; **w** (+ acc.) (*a game*) OR **na** (+ loc.) (*an instrument*)
play (2)	**bawić się** *-wię -wisz*; pf. **pobawić się** (*amuse oneself*)
please	**podobać się** *-am -asz*; pf. **spodobać się**; usually 3rd-person (+ dat.)

point	**wskazywać** *-zuję -zujesz*; pf. **wskazać** *-żę -żesz*; **na** (+ acc.) (*indicate*)
poke	**szturchać** *-am -asz*; pf. **szturchnąć** *-nę -niesz*
possess	**posiadać** *-am -asz*; pf. **posiąść** *-siądę -siądziesz*
pour	**lać** *leję lejesz*; pf. **nalać**
practice	**ćwiczyć się** *-czę -czysz*; pf. **poćwiczyć się**
precede	**poprzedzać** *-am -asz*; pf. **poprzedzić** *-dzę -dzisz*
prefer	**woleć** *-lę -lisz* (+ inf.)
prepare	**przygotowywać** *-wuję -wujesz*; pf. **przygotować** *-tuję -tujesz*
press	**naciskać** *-am -asz*; pf. **nacisnąć** *-snę -śniesz*
pretend	**udawać** *udaję udajesz*; pf. **udać** *udam udasz udadzą*
prick, sting	**kłuć** *-uję -ujesz*; pf. **ukłuć**
print	**drukować** *-kuję -kujesz*; pf. **wydrukować**
protect	**ochraniać** *-am -asz*; pf. **ochronić** *-nię -nisz*
pull	**ciągnąć** *-nę -niesz*; pf. **pociągnąć**
pull out	**wyciągać** *-am -asz*; pf. **wyciągnąć** *-nę -niesz* (*extract*)
punish	**karać** *-rzę -rzesz*; pf. **ukarać**
push	**popychać** *-am -asz*; pf. **popchnąć** *-nę -niesz* imp. *popchnij*
put (1)	**kłaść** *kładę kładziesz* past *kładł kładła kładli*; pf. **położyć** *-żę -żysz* imp. *połóż*
put (2)	**stawiać** *-am -asz*; pf. **postawić** *-wię -wisz* (*put in a standing position*)
put (3)	**umieszczać** *-am -asz*; pf. **umieścić** *-szczę -ścisz* (*place*)
put away, hide	**chować** *-am -asz*; pf. **schować**
put in	**wstawiać** *-am -asz*; pf. **wstawić** *-wię -wisz* (*insert*)
put on	**wkładać** *-am -asz*; pf. **włożyć** *-żę -żysz* imp. *włóż* (*clothes*)
quit (1)	**przestawać** *-staję -stajesz* imp. *przestawaj*; pf. **przestać** *-stanę -staniesz* imp. *przestań*; + inf. (*cease*)
quit (2)	**rezygnować** *-nuję -nujesz*; pf. **zrezygnować**; **z** (+ gen.) (*give up on*)
quit (3)	**rzucać** *-am -asz*; pf. **rzucić** *-cę -cisz* (*cast aside, give up* (e.g., *smoking*))
race	**ścigać się** *-am -asz*

raise (1)	**podnosić** *-noszę -nosisz*; pf. **podnieść** *-niosę -niesiesz* past *podniósł podniosła podnieśli* (*lift*)
raise (2)	**hodować** *-duję -dujesz*; pf. **wyhodować** (*animals, crops*)
raise (3)	**podwyższać** *-am -asz*; pf. **podwyższyć** *-szę -szysz* (*elevate*)
read	**czytać** *-am -asz*; pf. **przeczytać**
realize (1)	**zdawać sobie sprawę** *zdaję zdajesz*; pf. **zdać sobie sprawę** *zdam zdasz zdadzą*; z (+ gen.) (*learn*)
realize (2)	**realizować** *-zuję -zujesz*; pf. **zrealizować** (*bring to fruition*)
recall (1)	**przypominać sobie** *-am -asz*; pf. **przypomnieć sobie** *-mnę -mnisz* (*recollect*)
recall (2)	**odwoływać** *-łuję -łujesz*; pf. **odwołać** *-am -asz* (*rescind*)
receive	**otrzymywać** *-muję -mujesz*; pf. **otrzymać** *-am -asz*
recognize (1)	**poznawać** *-znaję -znajesz*; pf. **poznać** *-am -asz* (*recognize as familiar*)
recognize (2)	**uznawać** *-naję -najesz*; pf. **uznać** *-am -asz*; za (+ acc.) (*give recognition to someone for an achievement*)
recommend	**polecać** *-am -asz*; pf. **polecić** *-cę -cisz*
regret	**żałować** *-łuję -łujesz*; pf. **pożałować**; (+ gen.)
relate	**odnosić się** *-noszę -nosisz*; pf. **odnieść się** *-niosę -niesiesz* past *odniósł odniosła odnieśli*; do (+ gen.) *to*
relax, rest	**odpoczywać** *-am -asz*; pf. **odpocząć** *-cznę -czniesz*; imp. *odpocznij*
release	**wypuszczać** *-am -asz*; pf. **wypuścić** *-szczę -ścisz*
remove	**usuwać** *-am -asz*; pf. **usunąć** *-nę -niesz* (*eliminate*)
rent	**wynajmować** *-muję -mujesz*; pf. **wynająć** *-jmę -jmiesz*
repeat	**powtarzać** *-am -asz*; pf. **powtórzyć** *-rzę -rzysz*
replace (1)	**zastępować** *-puję -pujesz*; pf. **zastąpić** *-pię -pisz* (*take the place of*)
replace (2)	**zamieniać** *-am -asz*; pf. **zamienić** *-nię -nisz* imp. *zamień*; na (+ acc.) (*exchange for*)
request	**prosić** *-szę -sisz*; pf. **poprosić**; o (+ acc.) (*ask for*)
require	**wymagać** *-am -asz*; (+ gen.)
result	**wynikać** *-am -asz*; pf. **wyniknąć** *-nę -niesz*; usually 3rd-person; z (+ gen.) *from*

return	**wracać** *-am -asz*; pf. **wrócić** *-cę -cisz*
ride	**jeździć** *-żdżę -ździsz* imp. *jeźdź* (indet.); det. **jechać** *jadę jedziesz* imp. *jedź*; pf. **pojechać**
ripen	**dojrzewać** *-am -asz*; pf. **dojrzeć** *-rzeję -rzejesz*
risk	**ryzykować** *-kuję -kujesz*; pf. **zaryzykować**
rub	**trzeć** *trę trzesz* past *tarł tarła tarli* imp. *trzyj*
ruin	**psuć** *-uję -ujesz*; pf. **zepsuć** OR **popsuć**; intr. — **się**
run (1) ₋	**biegać** *-am -asz* (indet.); det. **biec** OR **biegnąć** *biegnę biegniesz* past *biegł biegła biegli* imp. *biegnij*; pf. **pobiec** (*sprint, flow*)
run (2)	**chodzić** *-dzę -dzisz* imp. *chodź* (*of machinery*). See go (1).
run (3)	**ubiegać się** *-am -asz*; **o** (+ acc.) (*be a candidate for*)
sail	**pływać** *-am -asz* (indet.); det. **płynąć** *-nę -niesz*; pf. **popłynąć**
satisfy	**zadowalać** *-am -asz*; pf. **zadowolić** *-lę -lisz* (+ dat.)
save (1)	**ratować** *-tuję -tujesz*; pf. **uratować** (*rescue*)
save (2)	**oszczędzać** *-am -asz*; pf. **oszczędzić** *-dzę -dzisz* (*economize*)
save (3)	**zachowywać** *-wuję -wujesz*; pf. **zachować** *-am -asz* (*preserve*)
say	**mówić** *-wię -wisz*; pf. **powiedzieć** *-wiem -wiesz -wiedzą* imp. *powiedz*
scare	**wystraszać** *-am -asz*; pf. **wystraszyć** *-szę -szysz* OR **przestraszać** OR **przestraszyć**
search for, seek	**szukać** *-am -asz*; pf. **poszukać** OR **znaleźć**; (+ gen.) (*see also find*)
see	**widzieć** *-dzę -dzisz*; pf. **zobaczyć** *-czę -czysz*
seem	**wydawać się** *-daję -dajesz*; pf. **wydać się** *-da -dadzą*; usually 3rd-person (+ dat.)
sell	**sprzedawać** *-daję -dajesz* imp. *sprzedawaj*; pf. **sprzedać** *-dam -dasz -dadzą* imp. *sprzedaj*
send (1)	**posyłać** *-am -asz*; pf. **posłać** *poślę poślesz* imp. *poślij*
send (2)	**wysyłać** *-am -asz*; pf. **wysłać** *wyślę wyślesz* imp. *wyślij* (*send off/away*)
serve (1)	**podawać** *-daję -dajesz* imp. *podawaj*; pf. **podać** *-dam -dasz -dadzą* imp. *podaj* (*dinner, a ball in tennis*)

serve (2)	**służyć -żę -żysz**; (+ dat.) (*aid*; also, *as a soldier in the army*)
set (1)	**ustalać -am -asz**; pf. **ustalić -lę -lisz** (*determine, fix*)
set (2)	**nastawiać -am -asz**; pf. **nastawić -wię -wisz** (*a clock*)
set (3)	**zachodzić -dzę -dzisz**; pf. **zajść -jdę -jdziesz** past **zaszedł zaszła zaszli** (*go down, as the sun*)
set off/out	**wyruszać -am -asz**; pf. **wyruszyć -szę -szysz** OR **wybierać się -am -asz**; pf. **wybrać się -biorę -bierzesz**
sew	**szyć -yję -yjesz**; pf. **uszyć**
shake (1)	**trząść się trzęsę trzęsiesz** past **trząsł trzęsła trząśli**; pf. **zatrząść się** (*tremble*)
shake (2)	**wstrząsać -am -asz**; pf. **wstrząsnąć -snę -śniesz** past **wstrząsnął wstrząsnęła wstrząsnęli**
share	**dzielić się -lę -lisz**; pf. **podzielić się**; (+ instr.)
shave	**golić -lę -lisz**; pf. **ogolić**; refl. — **się**
shine	**świecić (się) -cę -cisz**
shoot	**strzelać -am -asz**; pf. **strzelić -lę -lisz** OR **zastrzelić -lę -lisz** (*kill*)
shout	**krzyczeć -czę -czysz**; pf. **krzyknąć -nę -niesz**
show	**pokazywać -zuję -zujesz**; pf. **pokazać -żę -żesz**
shut	**zamykać -am -asz**; pf. **zamknąć -nę -niesz**; intr. — **się** (*also, lock*)
sign	**podpisywać -suję -sujesz**; pf. **podpisać -szę -szesz**
sing	**śpiewać -am -asz**; pf. **zaśpiewać**
sit	**siedzieć -dzę -dzisz**; pf. **posiedzieć**
sit down	**siadać -am -asz**; pf. **usiąść usiądę usiądziesz** past **usiadł usiadła usiedli** imp. **usiądź**
sleep	**spać śpię śpisz**; pf. **pospać**
slip	**poślizgać się -am -asz**; pf. **pośliznąć się -nę -niesz**
smell (1)	**czuć -uję -ujesz**; pf. **poczuć** (*sense*)
smell (2)	**pachnąć -nę -niesz** (*emit smell*)
smile	**uśmiechać się -am -asz**; pf. **uśmiechnąć się -nę -niesz**; **do** (+ gen.) at
smoke (1)	**dymić się -mię -misz**; usually 3rd-person (*emit smoke, as a chimney*)

smoke (2)	**palić** *-lę -lisz* (*use tobacco*)
smoke (3)	**wędzić** *-dzę -dzisz*; pf. **uwędzić** (*cure meats*)
sneeze	**kichać** *-am -asz*; pf. **kichnąć** *-nę -niesz*
solve	**rozwiązywać** *-zuję -zujesz*; pf. **rozwiązać** *-żę -żesz*
speak	**mówić** *-wię -wisz*. *See* say.
spend (1)	**spędzać** *-am -asz*; pf. **spędzić** *-dzę -dzisz* (*time*)
spend (2)	**wydawać** *-daję -dajesz*; pf. **wydać** *-dam -dasz -dadzą* imp. *wydaj* (*money*)
spill	**wylewać** *-am -asz*; pf. **wylać** *-leję -lejesz*; intr. — **się**
spit	**pluć** *-uję -ujesz*; pf. **plunąć** *-nę -niesz*
spoil	**psuć** *-uję -ujesz*; pf. **zepsuć** OR **popsuć** (*ruin*); intr. — **się**
stand	**stać** *stoję stoisz* imp. *stój*; pf. **postać**
stand up	**wstawać** *wstaję wstajesz*; pf. **wstać** *wstanę wstaniesz* imp. *wstań* (*arise*)
start	**zaczynać** *-am -asz*; pf. **zacząć** *-cznę -czniesz* imp. *zacznij*; intr. — **się**
stay	**zostawać** *-staję -stajesz*; pf. **zostać** *-stanę -staniesz* imp. *zostań* (*remain*)
steal	**kraść** *kradnę kradniesz* past *kradł kradła kradli* imp. *kradnij*; pf. **ukraść**
stink	**śmierdzieć** *-dzi*; usually 3rd-person
stop (1)	**zatrzymywać** *-muję -mujesz*; pf. **zatrzymać** *-am -asz*; intr. — **się** (*halt*)
stop (2)	**przestawać** *-staję -stajesz* imp. *przestawaj*; pf. **przestać** *-stanę -staniesz* imp. *przestań*; + inf. (*stop doing*)
strike (1)	**uderzać** *-am -asz*; pf. **uderzyć** *-rzę -rzysz* (*hit*)
strike (2)	**strajkować** *-kuję -kujesz*; pf. **zastrajkować** (*stage a strike*)
study (1)	**badać** *-am -asz*; pf. **zbadać** (*examine*)
study (2)	**studiować** *-diuję -diujesz*; pf. **przestudiować** (*be a student of*)
study (3)	**uczyć się** *uczę uczysz* (*try to learn*); pf. **nauczyć się** (*learn*)
subtract	**odejmować** *-muję -mujesz*; pf. **odjąć** *odejmę odejmiesz* imp. *odejmij*

succeed	**udawać się** *udaje*; pf. **udać się** *uda*; 3sg. only (+ dat.)
suck	**ssać** *ssę ssiesz* imp. *ssij*
suffer	**cierpieć** *-pię -piesz*; pf. **ucierpieć**
suggest	**sugerować** *-ruję -rujesz*; pf. **zasugerować**
suppose	**przypuszczać** *-am -asz*; pf. **przypuścić** *-szczę -ścisz*
swear (1)	**kląć** *klnę klniesz* imp. *klnij*
swear (2)	**przysięgać** *-am -asz*; pf. **przysięgnąć** *-nę -niesz* (*vow*)
sweep	**zamiatać** *-am -asz*; pf. **zamieść** *-miotę -mieciesz* past *zamiótł zamiotła zamietli*
swim	**pływać** *-am -asz* (indet.); det. **płynąć** *-nę -niesz*; pf. **popłynąć**
take (1)	**brać** *biorę bierzesz*; pf. **wziąć** *wezmę weźmiesz* imp. *weź* (*grasp, assume*)
take (2)	**zdawać** *zdaję zdajesz* (*take an exam*); pf. **zdać** *zdam zdasz zdadzą* (*pass an exam*)
take (3)	**zabierać** *-am -asz*; pf. **zabrać** *-biorę -bierzesz* (*take along*)
take care of (1)	**załatwiać** *-am -asz*; pf. **załatwić** *-wię -wisz* (*handle*)
take care of (2)	**opiekować się** *-kuję -kujesz*; pf. **zaopiekować się**; (+ instr.) (*care for*)
take off	**zdejmować** *-muję -mujesz*; pf. **zdjąć** *zdejmę zdejmiesz* imp. *zdejmij* (*clothes*)
talk	**rozmawiać** *-am -asz*; pf. **porozmawiać** (*converse*)
taste (1)	**smakować** *-kuję -kujesz*; usually 3rd-person, intr. (+ dat.)
taste (2)	**kosztować** *-tuję -tujesz*; pf. **skosztować** OR **zakosztować**; (+ gen.) (*try food*)
tear	**drzeć** *drę drzesz* past *darł darła darli* imp. *drzyj*; pf. **podrzeć**
tell	**opowiadać** *-am -asz*; pf. **opowiedzieć** *-wiem -wiesz -wiedzą*; imp. *opowiedz*; (+ dat.) (*narrate*). See say.
thank	**dziękować** *-kuję -kujesz*; pf. **podziękować**; (+ dat.)
think	**myśleć** *-lę -lisz* imp. *myśl*; pf. **pomyśleć**
throw	**rzucać** *-am -asz*; pf. **rzucić** *-cę -cisz*
tie	**wiązać** *-żę -żesz*; pf. **zawiązać** OR **związać**
translate	**tłumaczyć** *-czę -czysz*; pf. **przetłumaczyć**

travel	**podróżować** *-żuję -żujesz*
treat (1)	**leczyć** *-czę -czysz*; pf. **wyleczyć** (*heal*)
treat (2)	**traktować** *-tuję -tujesz*; pf. **potraktować** (*deal with*)
treat (3)	**częstować** *-tuję -tujesz*; pf. **poczęstować**; (+ acc./instr.) (*offer*)
trick	**oszukiwać** *-kuję -kujesz*; pf. **oszukać** *-am -asz*
trust	**ufać** *-am -asz*; pf. **zaufać**; (+ dat.)
try (1)	**próbować** *-buję -bujesz*; pf. **spróbować** (*test, taste*)
try (2)	**starać się** *-am -asz*; pf. **postarać się**; (+ inf.) (*attempt*)
turn, twist	**skręcać** *-am -asz*; pf. **skręcić** *-cę -cisz*
turn off	**wyłączać** *-am -asz*; pf. **wyłączyć** *-czę -czysz* (*disconnect*)
turn on	**włączać** *-am -asz*; pf. **włączyć** *-czę -czysz* (*an appliance*)
turn out	**okazywać się** *-zuję -zujesz*; pf. **okazać się** *-żę -żesz* (*appear*)
turn up	**pojawiać się** *-am -asz*; pf. **pojawić się** *-wię -wisz* (*appear*)
understand	**rozumieć** *-em -esz* imp. *rozum*; pf. **zrozumieć**
undress	**rozbierać** *-am -asz*; pf. **rozebrać** *rozbiorę rozbierzesz*; refl. — **się**
use	**używać** *-am -asz*; pf. **użyć** *-yję -yjesz*; (+ gen.) OR **korzystać** *-am -asz*; pf. **skorzystać**; **z** (+ gen.) (*make use of*)
visit (1)	**odwiedzać** *-am -asz*; pf. **odwiedzić** *-dzę -dzisz* (*pay a visit to*)
visit (2)	**zwiedzać** *-am -asz*; pf. **zwiedzić** *-dzę -dzisz* (*visit a place*)
vow	**ślubować** *-buję -bujesz*
wait	**czekać** *-am -asz*; pf. **poczekać** OR **zaczekać**; **na** (+ acc.) *for*
wake up	**budzić** *-dzę -dzisz*; pf. **obudzić** OR **zbudzić**; intr. — **się**
walk	**chodzić** *-dzę -dzisz*; det. **iść** *idę idziesz* past *szedł szła szli* imp. *idź*
want	**chcieć** *chcę chcesz*; pf. **zechcieć** imp. *zechciej*
warm	**grzać** *grzeję grzejesz*; pf. **zagrzać**
wash (1)	**myć** *myję myjesz*; pf. **umyć**; refl. — **się**
wash (2)	**prać** *piorę pierzesz*; pf. **wyprać** (*launder*)
waste (1)	**marnować** *-nuję -nujesz*; pf. **zmarnować** (*ruin*)

waste (2)	**tracić** *-cę -cisz*; pf. **stracić** (*time, money*)
watch	**oglądać** *-am -asz*; pf. **obejrzeć** *-rzę -rzysz* imp. *obejrzyj*
wave	**machać** *-am -asz*; pf. **machnąć** *-nę -niesz*; (+ instr.)
wed	**poślubiać** *-am -asz*; pf. **poślubić**
weigh	**ważyć** *-żę -żysz* (tr. or intr.); pf. **zważyć** (tr.)
win	**wygrywać** *-am -asz*; pf. **wygrać** *-am -asz*
wipe off	**wycierać** *-am -asz*; pf. **wytrzeć** *-trę -trzesz* past *wytarł wytarła wytarli* imp. *wytrzyj*
wish	**życzyć** *-czę -czysz*; pf. **zażyczyć** (+ gen.)
wonder	**zastanawiać się** *-am -asz*; pf. **zastanowić się** *-wię -wisz* imp. *zastanów;* **nad** (+ instr.) *at* (*consider*)
work (1)	**pracować** *-cuję -cujesz*; pf. **popracować** (*be employed*)
work (2)	**działać** *-am -asz* (*of an appliance*)
work out (1)	**rozwiązywać** *-zuję -zujesz*; pf. **rozwiązać** *-żę -żesz* (*solve*)
work out (2)	**trenować** *-nuję -nujesz*; pf. **potrenować** (*train*)
worry	**martwić** *-wię -wisz*; pf. **zmartwić** (*worry about*); — **się o** (+ acc.) (*be worried about*)
write	**pisać** *-szę -szesz*; pf. **napisać**
yawn	**ziewać** *-am -asz*; pf. **ziewnąć** *-nę -niesz*
yell	**krzyczeć** *-czę -czysz*; pf. **krzyknąć** *-nę -niesz* imp. *krzyknij*

Index